Narcissistic Abuse Recovery

A Guide to Breaking Free from Gaslighting, Manipulation, and Emotional Abuse, and Becoming Whole Again

acknowledge that the author is not engaged in the rendering of legal, financial, medical or professional advice. The content within this book has been derived from various sources. Please consult a licensed professional before attempting any techniques outlined in this book.

By reading this document, the reader agrees that under no circumstances is the author responsible for any losses, direct or indirect, that are incurred as a result of the use of the information contained within this document, including, but not limited to, errors, omissions, or inaccuracies.

Table of Contents

Your Free Gift

As a way of saying thanks for your purchase, I want to offer you a free bonus e-Book called *7 Essential Mindfulness Habits* exclusive to the readers of this book.

To get instant access, just go to:

https://theartofmastery.com/mindfulness

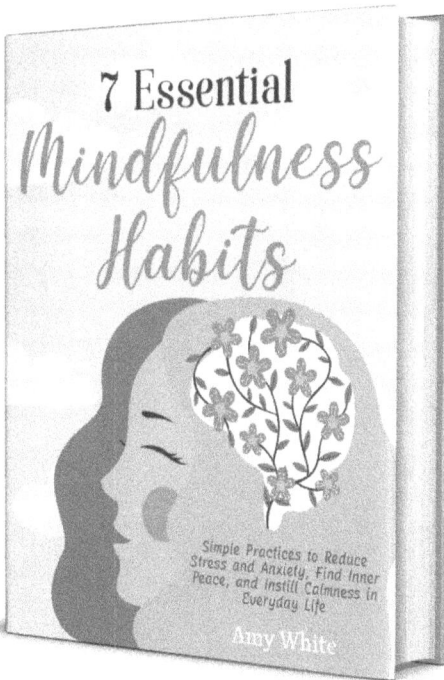

Inside the book, you will discover:

- What is mindfulness meditation?

- Why mindfulness is so effective in reducing stress and increasing joy, composure, and serenity
- Various mindfulness techniques that you can do anytime, anywhere
- 7 essential mindfulness habits to implement starting today
- Tips and fun activities to teach your kids to be more mindful

Introduction

"The lion is most handsome when looking for food." ~ *Rumi*

Do you justify staying in an unhealthy relationship because you are hoping that things will get better? What about when your partner verbally abuses you? Do you tell yourself that he/she is just having a bad day? Everyone who has suffered at the hands of a narcissist can relate to those sleepless nights spent searching your mind for answers. Deep down in the pit of your gut, you know that your union is wrong on so many levels, but you feel trapped. And instead of facing the reality of your situation, you protect yourself by living in denial and wishing upon a star that one day your narcissistic partner will go back to the sweet, loving, and caring person he/she was when you first started dating. NEWS FLASH! That's probably never going to happen because narcissists rarely change.

I've been in relationships with narcissists since I started dating. Unfortunately, I ended up marrying one, and they were the worst ten years of my life. By the time he was done with me, I felt like a hollow shell with nothing left to give. I had hit past rock bottom, and I didn't know how I was going to pick myself up.

Today, I am a thriving author with a BS in psychology. I chose to study this degree because after what I'd been through, I wanted to get a better understanding of the mind, how we think, and why we do the things that we do. Although I had spent years in therapy, educating myself took me to another level. It gave me full clarity on narcissistic personality disorder, and I really needed this to break free from bitterness so that I could fully forgive my ex-husband. I will never justify abuse, but narcissists are not born, they're made. It's not something they chose. It's difficult to separate the person from the disorder because most people who have been victims of narcissistic abuse are not aware that it's a personality disorder. Despite their grandiose outward appearance, narcissists are desperately insecure because of traumatic childhood experiences such as neglect or abuse, unrealistic parental expectations, or excessive parental pampering. Your abusive partners are victims too, and once you accept this, you will find it in your heart to have compassion for them so that you can move on with your life. Remember, hurt people hurt people, and that's why you became a victim of narcissistic abuse.

An important part of the healing process is forgiveness, and you won't fully heal unless you can forgive your partner. Unforgiveness leaves a sour taste in your mouth. You physically left the relationship months or even years ago, but your mind is still there, replaying everything that happened to you and wishing your ex-partner's life would end up in the trash heap the way yours has. Healing is a process; it takes time to recover from the wounds that have been inflicted upon your soul. Narcissists rob you of your joy, peace, sanity, and every bit of goodness you possess. In this book, you will learn about:

- Narcissistic personality disorder, the different categories of narcissists, and their character traits.
- The stages of narcissistic abuse
- Why you attract narcissists and how to get out of a relationship with one
- How to heal from narcissistic abuse and never get into a relationship with a narcissist again

During this healing process, you will learn a lot about yourself, your strengths, your weaknesses—but ultimately, you'll become a wiser, better, and grateful person for the experience. When you invest time in overcoming the emotional trauma you've suffered, you will eventually be able to tell the same story I'm telling: a tale of tenacity and resilience, knowing that you not only escaped from the clutches of a narcissist, you grew wings and learned how to soar!

Chapter 1: Know Thine Enemy – What is Narcissistic Personality Disorder?

"Red flags – ignoring them may be detrimental to your health and your sanity."

~ Anne McCrea

Narcissism is a spectrum disorder, which means there are levels to the condition. Some experts argue that we all have a bit of narcissism in us, and when you evaluate the traits, you can see why. However, people with narcissistic personality disorder (NPD) actually suffer from a psychological illness. According to the American Psychiatric Association (APA), narcissistic personality disorder is defined as: *"An excessive desire for admiration, delusions of grandiose and a lack of empathy."* The APA criteria state that psychologists should diagnose a person with NPD if they display five or more of the following characteristics:

- ✓ Grandiose and superior behavior
- ✓ Has fantasies about beauty, brilliance, power, success, or ideal love
- ✓ Believes they are so special that they should only associate with high-status people
- ✓ Expects constant admiration and praise

- ✓ An attitude of entitlement
- ✓ An explosive temper
- ✓ Lacks emotional empathy
- ✓ Always jealous of others
- ✓ Believes others are always jealous of him/her
- ✓ Haughty and arrogant

Let's go into a bit more depth about these character traits:

Grandiose and Superior: Deep down, narcissists are terribly insecure and cover it up by convincing themselves and others that they are superior beings and deserve to be treated as such. They look down on people and devalue anyone they feel will threaten their position.

Excessive Fantasies: Narcissists are perfectionists. They live out their extreme ideals in their imagination. They believe they are the most beautiful, powerful, and successful people in the world. Narcissists also have very unrealistic ideals about romantic love.

Believe They are Special: Narcissists don't like being put in the category of ordinary. As far as they are concerned, they are superior beings who should only associate with other superior beings.

Expect Admiration: Their deep need for external validation drives narcissists to seek excessive admiration and praise from outside sources. I will discuss narcissistic supply in a later section. Nevertheless, it revolves around them using others to feed their insecurities with worship. You can't be connected to a narcissist if you don't bow down to their needs. Anyone who does not lavish them with compliments is discarded.

An Attitude of Entitlement: You can't say no to a narcissist. They truly believe their friends and family members are to be at their beck and call at all times. When out in public, they expect to be treated like royalty. A narcissist should be given the best table at restaurants, the best seat at a concert, and the best deals when they go shopping. If not, the narcissist will cause a scene, lash out, or sulk because they genuinely believe they have been hard done by.

My ex-partner and I traveled a lot; wherever we went, Steven always insisted on booking 5-star hotels, and when we got there, he expected VIP treatment. We would unpack all our stuff, and within a few minutes, he would decide he doesn't like the room and ask to be moved. He would insist that the hotel staff walk him round to different rooms to see which one he preferred. If he felt he wasn't getting the service he deserved, he would become very aggressive and demanding.

Steven had no tolerance for smells and noise; he would get infuriated over the smell of food at restaurants, a baby crying, and the sound of the air conditioning. If he wasn't happy with the table we were given at a restaurant, he demanded we were moved.

An Explosive Temper: If a narcissist doesn't get what they want, or they feel that someone else is threatening their self-worth or self-esteem, they go crazy. Experts have termed this "narcissistic rage," I will discuss it fully in another section.

Lacks Emotional Empathy: Narcissists don't connect emotionally with people, which is why they find it so easy to abuse their partners. They believe that the people in their lives only have one purpose, and that is to serve them no matter what it costs these individuals.

Jealousy: If a narcissist is not the center of attention, they get extremely jealous. A person is considered a threat to a narcissist if they are more attractive, funnier, drive a better car, have a better job, or a prettier girlfriend; basically, anyone who threatens their inflated sense of self-worth, they envy. Narcissists also believe that others are jealous of them and that they are trying to take what belongs to them. This often leads to false accusations and paranoia.

Haughty and Arrogant: Narcissists always want to be at the top of the food chain. This drives them to be competitive, punishing, or explosive in behavior if they feel that someone is trying to take their spot. They also engage in excessive gloating, gossiping, bragging, ridiculing, name dropping, correcting, and condescending behavior.

More Narcissistic Traits

As well as the traits described by the APA, there are other important psychological aspects of narcissistic personality disorder you should know about to give you a better understanding of the condition.

Shame: Underneath the narcissist's well-constructed armor of defense is an emotionally unstable child who feels unworthy and ashamed. You see, as much as we love to hate narcissists, they didn't choose to be this way. When children are not given the developmental support they need to become emotionally stable adults, it causes mental illness. What narcissists are really looking for is love, and their defense mechanism of self-deception is their way of preventing psychological collapse. They must feel superior to others to keep them from feeling the shame they've buried. Narcissists are at war with no one but themselves, and this internal dilemma causes them to have tumultuous relationships. Their feelings of self-hatred are so intense that they reject them through projection. The person closest to them is subjected to their inner wrath because they so desperately need someone in their life to carry the burden of the hatred they feel for themselves.

Attention Seeking: You will find a lot of narcissists within the entertainment industry because it provides them with the attention they so desperately crave. It is normal to want a certain level of admiration and for your gifts and talents to be admired. But the need that the narcissist has is excessive, and they will get it by any means necessary. Figuratively speaking, narcissists suck all the oxygen out of any room they are in. Depending on the type of narcissist they are (we will get into that later), they will dominate social arenas with exhibitionist or passive-aggressive behavior.

Emotionally Reactive: Narcissists are emotionally reactive and hyper-defensive because of their delusions of grandiosity. Their reactivity manifests in a number of ways, such as rage, blaming, intolerance, huffiness, and haughtiness. This behavior is worsened by their lack of emotional empathy, which makes it so easy for the narcissist to punish, hurt, and judge others.

Distorted Self-Beliefs: Psychologists have described narcissists as having distorted self-beliefs that fluctuate between extreme entitlement, and superiority, and self-hatred. They are constantly fighting to manage their self-esteem and are desperately dependent on others to give them the reassurance they can't give themselves. Narcissists are very sensitive to criticism, even if it's constructive, because their defenses are structured around the belief that they are superior and privileged.

Constructive criticism leads to outbursts because they have no social awareness. For this reason, you will often find that narcissists find it difficult to keep a job.

In the ten years I was with Steve, he had about two jobs a year because he could never get past the probationary period. Normal people understand that in most places of employment, they give you a permanent position after you've proved yourself. During this probationary period, your managers and supervisors are monitoring your work ethic and attitude. If there is anything they think you can improve on, they will tell you during the evaluation meeting. Steve would either come home absolutely infuriated that someone he thought was beneath him (because he always believed he could do a better job) had the audacity to point out that he needed to work on something such as his punctuation. May I add that Steve was always late because he was too busy primping in the mirror! This was just evidence of his lack of self-awareness. Another one of his strategies was that he would quit the job shortly before the probationary period was over because, deep down, he knew his performance was less than perfect, and he didn't want to hear the criticism.

Superficial Relationships: You will rarely meet a narcissist who has a childhood friend or who is in a long-term committed relationship where the love and respect are mutual. No matter how long they are with a person, they will never commit. There are several reasons for this:

- **They Don't Trust Anyone:** To develop trust in a relationship, both partners must display a level of vulnerability. It requires exposing parts of yourself that you hide from the rest of the world, but you feel safe revealing to your significant other. Once you reveal this information, how that person reacts to it will determine whether you start trusting them or not. The problem with narcissists is that they view vulnerability as a sign of weakness, and since their image revolves around their imagined superiority, they will never reveal their true selves, which means they are incapable of trusting people.

- **Ulterior Motives:** The narcissist's main goal is narcissistic supply. The only reason why they want people in their lives is so they can give them what they need. As mentioned, they need praise and admiration, and one of their tactics (as you will soon read about) is to be extremely generous and giving so that the recipient is fooled into believing they are this wonderful, amazing person.

- **They Lack Empathy:** You can tell a narcissist that your mom just died, and they will skip right over what you've said to tell you about the new car they've purchased. They don't have the capacity to connect with people on an emotional level because everything is about them.

What the Narcissist Fears Most

Narcissists work overtime to ensure their true identity is never revealed. Every narcissistic abuse survivor knows that narcissists have three sides to their character: their public persona, the person their partner knows, and who they really are. This is a heavy weight to carry, and being found out that they are a fraud terrifies them. Here are some of their worst fears:

Being Humiliated: The grandiose and hypersensitive nature of the narcissist leads them to have unrealistic expectations. As a result, they are threatened by the tiniest slights that others would brush off. No one likes being humiliated and embarrassed, but it is the worst thing in the world to a narcissist because of their emotional instability. To avoid these feelings, when in a social setting, they preempt who they suspect might try and embarrass them, and they get in there first to ensure they keep their position. They have a tendency to compete about everything and will align themselves with whatever status symbols are within reach, such as:

- Having a better car
- Having smarter children

- Having the most successful friends
- Having more social media followers
- Living in a warmer climate
- Reading more academic literature
- Owning a larger TV screen
- Being more attractive
- Going on the best vacations

Being Exposed: Emotionally healthy people are very self-aware and want to be authentic at all times. They practice self-reflection and enjoy having intimate relationships with the people they care about. On the other hand, narcissists are terrified of exposure, and therefore avoid self-reflection. They do not seek intimacy because they see it as a threat. Narcissists don't know who they truly are because they work so hard to disguise their vulnerabilities by deluding themselves with a false sense of superiority. The most important thing to them is convincing everyone around them of their superiority. Narcissists are so unstable that they are totally dependent on external measures of self-worth. To get it, they coerce and manipulate friends, lovers, colleagues, and family members into believing the narrative surrounding their persona.

Being Rejected: Any form of rejection is the narcissist's worst fear because it triggers everything they work so hard to keep buried. Because of their deep sense of unlovability and inferiority, personal, professional, or social rejection is severely destabilizing and invalidating. People with a healthy sense of self see rejection as a stepping stone to success. In contrast, the narcissist will attempt to regain control by resorting to abuse. They have set their lives up to play the role of rejecter, and their strategy is to discard before being discarded. But if they don't get there first, they will pull out every weapon in their arsenal to take back their perceived loss of power.

Types of Narcissists

As well as narcissistic personality disorder, psychologists have also determined that there are variants of narcissists:

Malignant Narcissist: Some mental health experts have labeled malignant narcissism as a very severe subtype of the disorder. They typically display the following characteristics:

- **Sadism:** They take pleasure in inflicting pain on others; it makes them feel powerful. Malignant narcissists get excited about the vocal expression of pain from their victims, such as screaming, crying, or begging for mercy.
- **Anti-Social Personality:** Psychologists suggest that malignant narcissism is an offshoot

of anti-social personality disorder. It involves the exploitation and manipulation of others without remorse. They have no regard for what other people think about them and display very similar symptoms of sociopathy.

- **Malicious and Sophisticated Plotting:** Malignant narcissists are very calculated in everything they do, especially when it comes to revenge. A narcissist will just go off on a tangent, whereas a malignant narcissist spends a lot of time planning every aspect of their attack.

- **Aggression:** Although narcissists are not always physically violent, when malignant narcissists start believing they own their partners and see them as property, they are likely to turn very aggressive and violent.

- **Psychopathy:** Clinical psychologist Dr. Craig Malkin describes malignant narcissism as a combination of psychopathy and narcissism, characterized by the guiltless or remorseless treatment of others. It also displays traits of Machiavellianism, which is described as a heartless, chess-playing approach to love and life.

Covert Narcissist: Covert narcissism typically involves fewer external signs of classic narcissistic personality disorder, but they still meet the diagnosis criteria. Additionally, they have traits that are not typically associated with NPD, such as humility, shyness, and sensitivity to other people's opinions of them. However, in general, they display the following symptoms:

- **Passive Aggression:** At some point in our lives, we have all used passive aggression as a manipulation tactic. But covert narcissists use it as a tool to make themselves appear superior or communicate frustration. This behavior is driven by the fact that narcissists believe they are special and therefore entitled to get what they want. They also display passive aggression to get revenge on the people they believe have had more success than them or those who have offended them; it can manifest in the form of:

  ✓ Sabotaging a person's friendships or work
  ✓ Mocking or teasing remarks disguised as jokes
  ✓ Procrastinating on assignments they think they are too good for
  ✓ Subtly shifting the blame in a way that makes others question whether the incident really happened, or makes them feel bad

- **They Put Themselves Down:** People with covert narcissism do the opposite of what classic narcissists do and downgrade themselves in front of others instead of boosting themselves up. However, their aim is the same: the desire for compliments. In downplaying their contributions, they hope that the person they are talking to will give them the validation they are looking for. Or they will give people compliments for the sole purpose of getting one in return.

- **Withdrawn and Shy:** By keeping their social interactions to a minimum, the covert narcissist hopes to avoid exposing their deep-seated feelings of inferiority.

- **Grandiose Fantasies:** Instead of talking about their imaginary successes in life, they fantasize about them. Their attitude is a smug one of show and not tell, but the reality is that they aren't working towards anything. The covert narcissist withdraws into a fantasy world where they have inflated powers of importance; however, their real life is far from the narrative playing in their head. Their fantasies may involve:

  - ✓ Praise for being the hero
  - ✓ Admired for their attractiveness
  - ✓ Being promoted at work or recognized for their talents

- **They Hold Grudges:** When the covert narcissist feels they've been offended, they feel extremely angry but won't say anything. Instead, they will wait for the perfect opportunity to get revenge or make the other person look bad. They also hold grudges against the people who earn the recognition or praise they believe they should have got, such as a coworker who got a promotion because they worked extremely hard for it.

- **Self-Serving Empathy:** Covert narcissists appear to have empathy for others. They will extend a helping hand and make sacrifices to help others. You might see them giving food or money to a homeless person or offering to lend a friend their car. But they have an ulterior motive. They want to win the approval of the people they are helping, and if they don't get the admiration and praise they think they deserve for their acts of kindness, they become resentful and bitter and start talking about how people are ungrateful and taking advantage of them.

Overt Narcissist: They are the complete opposite of covert narcissists and carry around an intense air of entitlement. They are adrenaline junkies and exploitative. Like the classic narcissist, they are extremely insecure but parade high self-esteem as a cover-up. The overt narcissist has a very braggadocios attitude, and they are not afraid to put it on full display. They are arrogant, vain, and boastful and will say things like, "You are the one who needs *me*. I don't need you," or "I can have any woman I want." They do not depend on friends, family, or lovers and avoid getting close to people. Everyone is fooled into believing they are the devoted friend or attentive lover, and their social media accounts will make sure all posts promote the image they want to reinforce.

Grandiose narcissists get into a relationship for self-serving reasons such as connections, proper appearances, or power. It is a one-sided relationship where they expect to be pampered at all times. They place very high and unrealistic demands on their partners that are impossible to fulfill. When their significant other is unable to deliver, the consequence is aggressive abuse.

Sexual Narcissist: There is nothing wrong with having confidence in your sexual abilities. Neither is it a crime to focus on your own pleasure during intercourse. Sexual narcissists display these characteristics, but they also believe that they are entitled to sex whenever they want it when they are in a romantic relationship, and they will manipulate and exploit their partner to get it. They don't have sex for emotional connection but for physical pleasure and praise for their performance. The main symptoms of sexual narcissism include:

- Have a tantrum if they are refused sex
- Get offended if they don't feel their partner praised them enough for their performance
- Believe their sexual performance is superior
- Need a lot of admiration and validation for their sexual performance
- Not concerned with their partner's pleasure
- Willing to manipulate, deceive, or trick their partner into having sex
- Expect sex in return for favors or gifts
- Even if their partner is sleeping, working, or busy doing something else, they expect them to stop and have sex

Somatic Narcissist: They use their physical space and body to express their narcissism. The main symptoms of a somatic narcissist include:

- **Obsessed with Appearance:** They spend a lot of time obsessing over things that relate to the body, such as diet and exercise. Somatic narcissists are known to have a lot of plastic surgery. They also spend a lot of money on makeup, fitness equipment, and clothes. They do everything possible to make sure their outward appearance is pleasing to the eye. They also fish for compliments and brag about how they look.

- **Their Self Esteem is Based on Sex:** They only seek out trophy partners, they are never faithful, and have compulsive sexual behavior. Somatic narcissists also manipulate their partners for sex because, like sexual narcissists, their validation comes from feeling sexually attractive.

- **They Don't Like Ugly People:** Somatic narcissists are deeply offended by people they don't find attractive. Despite the fact that they must be the center of attention at all times, they only associate with people they deem as good-looking.

Cerebral Narcissist: Cerebral narcissists believe they are highly intelligent and spend a lot of time bragging about their intellectual capabilities. Symptoms of cerebral narcissism include:

- **The Desire to Appear Intellectual:** They can't have a normal conversation; their vocabulary is littered with words that require a dictionary to interpret. They find ways to talk about books, authors, and theories. Cerebral narcissists have the tendency to refer to their ideas as "cutting edge." They intimidate most people because they struggle to understand what they are saying. Listeners are either in awe of them, or they shut off because the cerebral narcissist is too difficult to understand.

- **Dominate Conversation:** They don't like listening to people and will cut off whoever they are speaking to because they believe what they've got to say is more important. Cerebral narcissists look bored or yawn during conversation because they perceive the speaker as uneducated and unqualified.

- **Elitist and Snobby:** A cerebral narcissist will mock people who either haven't had any education or went to a university they deem as inferior. If someone uses a big word during conversation, they will question them about the meaning in hopes of shaming them. They will brag about the university they attended and the degree they hold. A cerebral narcissist will look down on people who don't eat at upper-class restaurants or stay in 5-star hotels.

Now that you have a better understanding of narcissistic personality disorder, let's move on to patterns of narcissistic abuse.

Chapter 2: Patterns of Narcissistic Abuse

"Don't judge yourself by what others did to you." ~ *C. Kennedy*

Like other forms of emotional abuse, narcissistic abuse is also referred to as "invisible abuse." Unlike physical abuse, it is absent of bruises, cuts, or scratches. The bullying starts off very subtle and progresses to the more overt type. But it is very difficult for outsiders to spot. In fact, narcissistic abuse is so manipulative that even the victim can't identify it. In a lot of cases, the narcissist manages to convince them that they are too sensitive, they are imagining it, they are overreacting, or they are blamed for the abuse.

Signs of Narcissistic Abuse

The distinguishing feature of narcissistic abuse is that there is a pattern to it. Once the victim is out of the relationship, they can look back and pinpoint exactly how it played out. When I started my group therapy, I was amazed at how similar our stories were, even down to the vocabulary narcissists used.

Love-Bombing/Devalue/Discard: When I first met Steve, he was a dream come true. He met me when I was at the lowest point of my life. My dad had just died, and I was desperately looking for comfort. The dangerous thing about narcissists is that they are extremely charming, and they draw you in using a strategy called "love-bombing." It's a part of their two-pronged approach to hooking their victim:

- **Love-Bombing:** This is the most important part of the strategy because it's how they get you addicted to them. In the beginning, whoever the narcissist is dating will feel like they are in paradise. Steve swept me off my feet very quickly. He told me everything I needed to hear. I was the most beautiful woman in the world, he had never met anyone like me before, I was intelligent, brave, amazing. He wrote me long letters declaring his everlasting love for me. I got addicted to checking my phone first thing in the morning because he would send me a really sweet text message late at night, and my day would start off with butterflies in my stomach. Steve bought me expensive gifts, took me on vacation, and made sure I had everything I needed. He was extremely attentive and paid attention to every last detail of my personality. He knew my favorite color, favorite meal, and favorite movie, so everything he did for me was based on what he knew I liked. All my friends and family thought I was the luckiest woman in the world. I fell head over heels in love with him, and we moved in together within two months of meeting. He would say things like:

- "I'm going to marry you one day."
- "You're so perfect, beautiful, smart, kind, and creative."
- "All we need is each other."
- "You're my only friend. Am I your only friend?"
- "I've never had such strong feelings for anyone before."
- "The universe brought us together; we were meant to be."
- "No one else understands me like you do."

These words of affirmation quickly turned into sly, bitter insults, and I didn't see it coming, not even for a second.

- **Devalue:** Once he knew that he had me hooked, that I craved his endearing words, warmth, and affection, then came the devaluing stage. I was completely blinded by what was taking place, and many of you reading this will relate. I wondered if I was losing my mind, hearing things, I was constantly questioning myself.

Basically, I was in denial. It started with insults dressed up as compliments. One night I was getting ready to go to a friend's birthday dinner. He walked up behind me, kissed me on the neck, and whispered, "You're so beautiful, but you look fat in that dress," and then walked off as if he had done nothing wrong. I literally felt my heart drop into my stomach. I brushed it off because I didn't want to accept that he had just said something extremely cruel. I did a double take in the mirror. I hadn't put on any weight; I was the same size as when he met me, so maybe he just got a glimpse from the wrong angle. The next day, while we were lying in bed, he started rubbing my stomach in his usual affectionate way and said, "I loved that dress you were wearing yesterday, but when are you going on a diet?" I asked him if he thought I was putting on weight, and he said, "No, I just think it's important that we learn to take care of our health." He then swiftly changed the subject. Of course, I went on a diet the next day because I wanted to please him. But the more weight I lost, the more he kept telling me I was fat.

According to psychologist Matthew Crane, emotional abuse is like a drug. During the love-bombing stage, the reason why you feel like you're walking on clouds is because your brain is releasing a surge of the feel-good hormone dopamine into your system. It's the same process that drug addicts go through. Once the drugs wear off and dopamine stops flowing, they crash and go out in search of their next high. You will often hear addicts mention the term "chasing the high." That's because they are always trying to recreate the feeling they got from the first high. This process is what keeps emotional abuse victims stuck in a cycle of abuse. They get addicted to their partner's approval. They desperately want to reclaim the first few months of their relationship where they felt so good because their partner was so charming, so they do anything and everything to try and get back there.

I lost count of the number of times I changed my hairstyle from color to length to style because Steve would tell me he didn't like the way my hair looked. He would start off saying stuff like, "I prefer women with short hair," I would cut it, he would tell me I looked beautiful, and then a couple of weeks later, he would say, "I hate women with short hair," so I'd go out and get extensions. Then he didn't like brunettes, so I dyed my hair blonde, then he preferred darker hair, so I dyed it black. He was always saying things like:

- "You need psychological help."
- "You get offended too easily."
- "That's why you don't have any friends."
- "My friends can't stand you. They think I could do a lot better, but I always defend you."
- "You've got such low self-esteem."
- "Why are you acting like this?"
- "Why do you always put your friends before me?"
- "There's no point in crying because your tears have no effect on me."
- "You're such a manipulative person."

I was on an emotional roller coaster, and I didn't know whether I was coming or going. But all I knew was that I wanted to go back to the love we had at the start of the relationship, and I was willing to do anything to get there.

- **Discard:** Emotional abuse will suck the life out of you and completely destroy your sense of self. The narcissist has you in his life for one reason only, and that is to feed off your energy and act as a source of supply. Narcissistic supply is the attention and praise narcissists need to survive. It's the equivalent of heroin to an addict—no lie.

When a narcissist isn't getting praise and attention, it triggers a psychological reaction. It's important to mention here that they are not looking for insincere, halfhearted praise. There's got to be a certain energy behind it. That's why narcissists work so hard during the love-bombing phase. They are pouring energy into you so that you can pour it back into them. As far as they're concerned, your supply is a tradeoff. But during the devaluing phase, the narcissist strips you of every ounce of dignity you've ever had. Your emotional state is so unstable that you are fiercely in love with him, and at the same time, you hate him with every fiber of your being. Once you get to this point, you've got no energy left to praise the narcissist because you are fully aware of what he's done to you.

This is why I will stand by the fact that narcissism is a mental illness and not a calculated choice. Essentially, narcissism is biting the hand that feeds you. What the narcissist wants is supply. They want it from their victim, so why wear them down so much that they are no longer able to give it to you? It makes no logical sense, but there is no logic in mental illness. When the narcissist can no longer feed off your energy, they get rid of you. Discard can also happen when they realize you are on to them, as this is a threat to the false sense of self they've presented. Or, they've found a better option. Maybe they feel that person is not only better looking but willing to worship the ground they walk on in a way that you aren't.

The discard phase is the final part of the cycle, but more often than not, the relationship is not over. If the narcissist knows that ditching you will completely destroy you, they won't come back because they are satisfied that their job is done. In the narcissist's head, the fact that they were able to cause you so much emotional disturbance is evidence of how special they are. After they've walked out, and you keep texting, emailing, calling, and turning up at his workplace to find out what you did wrong to make him leave, such behavior is the narcissist's ultimate victory. You will know when the narcissist is getting ready to discard you because he will start saying things like:

- "The only reason why this relationship is coming to an end is because of you."
- "Enjoy the rest of your lonely and miserable life."

- "You will never find anyone better than me."
- "You're such a terrible person."
- "No one likes you, not even your own family."

Unless you're aware of the narcissist's relationship cycle, you'll have no idea he's getting ready to leave you. I didn't. I came back from work one day to find that he had moved out. He took all his clothes and everything he had bought with his money, which was practically everything. I was left with nothing but a roof over my head. He changed his phone number and blocked me on all social media platforms. Of course, I started stalking him. I went to his workplace, his mother's house, friends, and cousins trying to get answers; no one wanted to tell me anything.

Withholding: Withholding is a common narcissistic abuse tactic. It includes giving their victim the silent treatment, a sudden withdrawal of physical intimacy and affection, and random disappearing acts. I'm talking, they will just go missing in action for days, turn off their phone, refuse to reply to direct messages on social media or email. So you don't call the police, they'll get in touch with a friend or family member they know you'll contact when looking for them so that when you do call, they'll say, "Oh, I just spoke to him yesterday. I'm sure he's fine." And then, just as swiftly as they disappeared, they'll turn up again and act as if they've done absolutely nothing wrong. Steve would go as far as to lie and insist that he told me he was going on a trip with friends! The first time it happened, I spent hours arguing with him that he hadn't told me anything. His lie was so calculated that he gave me a date and an estimated time in which he informed me of this trip! The only way I could deal with the deceit was to convince myself that I must not have heard him.

Narcissists also withdraw by completely ignoring you at a social gathering but engaging with other guests. They'll be super friendly with them, too, because they know you're watching, which just rubs salt into the wound. Psychologists claim that withholding activates a response in the same part of the brain that registers physical pain. In other words, it feels like you've been sucker-punched in the gut!

Verbal Abuse: Some narcissists are so skilled at verbal abuse that they will actually convince you that their insults are helping you. The insults start slowly, the tone is mild, with very little abusive language. If you're lucky, you might get a shallow apology when you point out that your feelings have been hurt. Then they take it up a notch by shaming you in public, and the insults become a bit more frequent. Their tone becomes a bit more aggressive, and they will start blaming you for them having to insult you, but all in the same breath, they will deny they are abusing you!

Narcissists use the tone and volume of their voice to establish dominance on a subconscious level. They will either yell, scream, or rage or they will refuse to give you an answer, ignore you, or give you the silent treatment. The tone reinforces the fact that they are abusing you.

When Steve first started verbally abusing me, he wrapped it up in a joke. He would say things like, "You look really ugly today. Gosh, I didn't realize how atrocious-looking you were." My face would drop, then he would kiss me on the forehead and tell me it was only a joke. What normal person makes jokes like that? Whether disguised as a joke, game, teasing, or sarcasm, it's unacceptable and hurtful. This type of verbal abuse is difficult to recognize because of its undercover nature, but you'll catch it if you're paying attention. Here are some of the most common ways a narcissist verbally abuses his victims:

- **Blocking:** This is one of the many tactics narcissists use to shut down conversations they don't want to have. They will accuse you of something, switch topics, or use language that tells you to "shut up."

- **Denying:** The narcissist will deny they made promises or agreements with you or that events or a conversation took place. Instead, they might throw you off guard by making declarations of their undying love for you. Once you've been sucked into his web of deceit because you feel so good about how affectionate he's being, you'll convince yourself that maybe you heard wrong or that your experience or perception was a misunderstanding.

- **Interrupting and Undermining:** They will say things to undermine your confidence and self-esteem, such as, "Can you hear how stupid you sound?" Or, the narcissist will speak for you or finish your sentence without giving him permission.

- **Belittling and Discounting:** This style of verbal abuse trivializes or minimizes your thoughts, feelings, or experiences. It's a way of saying your feelings are either wrong or unimportant.

Toddler Tantrums: The narcissist feels that he is deserving of preferential or special treatment. They also believe that their needs should be met immediately, or all hell breaks loose. Have you ever been in the presence of a two-year-old denied candy by his mother at a store?

It's a terrible sight. They fling themselves on the floor, screaming while flailing their legs and arms all over the place. Anyone who walks by is likely to get a black eye or a kick in the knee! Well, when you refuse to give the narcissist what they want, that's what you'll get.

Slander: Hell have no fury like a narcissist scorned! If you think you can annoy a narcissist and get away with it, you are living in a bigger fantasy land than the narcissist. Steve was also a sexual narcissist. The very first time I refused to meet his sexual demands was the last time I ever said no. We were in a relationship, so I trusted him and allowed him to take some nude photos of me. He sent those pictures to all our mutual friends with the caption, *Imagine having all this and not being able to do anything with it.* Unbeknownst to me, he sent those pictures right in front of me while we were lying in bed. My phone started pinging off the hook about the nude they'd just received. I was mortified. Of course, he acted like it was a mistake, and he was meant to send it to me. He looked me right in the eye, and in the most menacing way, said, "Well, babe, it wouldn't have happened if you'd just said yes. Lucky I didn't send one to your dad." He then rolled over and went to sleep!

If you don't give the narcissist what they want, they will get their revenge by slandering your name in the worst way possible. They will also destroy your reputation if they think you're on to them (I'll talk about this later).

But the worst thing you can do to a narcissist is call them a narcissist. This means you know he's a fraud, and who they claim to be is not who they really are. That's the narcissist's worst fear, and as soon as those words come out of your mouth, he will launch his smear campaign against you.

Not Taking Responsibility: Taking responsibility for your actions is a form of personal accountability. It means looking within, being vulnerable with yourself, and admitting that you were wrong. The ability to be accountable for one's behavior is the most essential characteristic of a morally centered, mentally healthy, and responsible adult. This is how we grow and learn from our mistakes and live a life that reflects our value system. Most of us know the difference between right and wrong. We learn that from an early age. But narcissists find it incredibly difficult to confront their feelings, admit to their mistakes, and apologize.

One of the hallmarks of narcissistic personality disorder is the inability to take responsibility for their actions. If something goes wrong, they will turn it around on you and make it look like you're at fault. You're the crazy one and not them. If you've got evidence to back up what you're saying, such as a receipt or a text message, they'll outright deny it or say they don't remember. They'll say you misunderstood what was said and rewrite the narrative of what they were really trying to communicate. In this way, they don't need to take responsibility because you got it wrong, not them.

Why do they hate taking responsibility for their actions so much? As you have read, deep down, narcissists despise themselves. They are very fragile individuals who don't have a strong sense of self to rely on. They are already walking on unstable ground. For the average person, taking ownership and admitting we've made a mistake feels good. But because the narcissist isn't grounded in who they are, it feels better to pass the baton of responsibility on to someone else. In this way, they prevent experiencing the feelings of insecurity they are so afraid of. Narcissists can't handle being caught out in their mistakes because it opens the door to vulnerability, and that's a no-no for narcissists.

When you live with a narcissist, it's like walking on eggshells; you just don't know when they're going to strike. Everything is about saving and maintaining their own credibility, and they'll do whatever is necessary to achieve that.

Projecting: Another hallmark sign of narcissistic abuse is projection. I lost count of the number of times Steve accused me of cheating. If he thought I took too long when I went to the store, I was having an affair. If I happened to hang up the phone when he walked in the room, I was having an affair. If I laughed too much when I was online, I was having an affair. The accusations were ridiculous, but he had managed to convince me that it was because he loved me so much, and he was terrified of losing me. Narcissists project their behavior onto you because, in their fantasy world, they are perfect humans who can't step a foot wrong. It was not at all surprising that I found out he was cheating on me the entire time we were together. Here are some other ways narcissists project their foolishness onto you and other people:

- **Exaggeration/Mimicking/Grandiosity:**
  Narcissists think they're so special they deserve top-of-the-range treatment, or they're justified in being so cruel to other people. They set themselves unrealistic goals, and to appear more superior and impressive, they exaggerate their achievements. Narcissists feel the need to compete with everyone because, deep down, they know they're not as exceptional as they've made out to be. In an attempt to gain the upper hand, they'll exploit, hurt, lie, pretend, or do whatever else they think they need to do for personal gain. Narcissists have a tendency to take on other people's achievements and character traits. This comes from a place of self-aggrandizement and envy, often to the extent of being a fraud, stealing, plagiarizing, and mimicking—all while belittling and defaming others. If someone has

something the narcissist admires, instead of taking the necessary steps to achieve it, they lie that they've got it.

- **Playing the Victim:** Playing the victim is a common narcissistic strategy. Everything is "poor me," and despite the fact that they are the ones doing the abusing, they will tell the world they're the victim. This happened several times during my relationship with Steve. Once, after an argument, he called my mom, crying and screaming on the phone about how I was calling him stupid, dumb, and ugly because I didn't want him to go out with his friends. He did this in front of me, and I was outraged! He had just called me all these things because he didn't want me to go out with my friends! But the worst part is that my mom believed him, and so did everyone else to who he played the victim. Seriously, he should have won an Oscar for some of his performances.

Gaslighting: Gaslighting is the narcissist's ace card. This is what they do best. It's a form of emotional abuse that involves manipulating someone by forcing them to question their memories, thoughts, and the events surrounding them. The narcissist will twist the truth so well that you'll think you've lost your mind. I was fascinated to discover that the term gaslighting actually comes from a film called *Gaslight* where an abusive husband torments and manipulates his wife so much that he convinces her she's going mad.

According to Dr. Robin Stern, author of *The Gaslight Effect: How to Spot and Survive the Hidden Manipulation Others Use to Control Your Life,* signs that your partner is gaslighting you include:

- Feeling hopeless and no longer enjoying the activities you used to
- Finding it difficult to make decisions
- Feeling isolated from family and friends
- Avoiding being open with friends and family so you don't upset your partner
- Justifying your partner's behavior
- Questioning the way you respond to your partner
- Feeling that something isn't right, but you are unable to identify it
- Apologizing all the time
- Blaming yourself when things go wrong
- Concerned that you're being too sensitive
- Being less confident than you once were but more anxious than you've ever been
- Feeling like a shadow of your former self

Gaslighters are experts at getting a reaction out of you. They know your vulnerabilities and sensitivities, and they use that knowledge against you. As a victim of gaslighting, you will doubt yourself, question your memory, your judgment, and your sanity. Here are some classic examples of gaslighting:

- **Insisting you either did or didn't go to a certain place:** "You've lost your mind. You didn't come to my cousin's wedding with me; I would remember."

- **Hiding things from you:** "Why are you always losing things? You're so disorganized."

- **Denying things they've said:** "I didn't say I'd take the money to the bank, thanks a lot for getting us another overdraft fee."

- **Telling you people are talking about you:** "I'm surprised you didn't know your family is always saying nasty things about you. They don't understand why I'm even with you."

- **Trivializing your feelings:** "It's not that serious. Just get over it already."

Lying: Narcissists are completely shameless with their lies, and they will do or say anything to get the desired result. They enjoy lying because they don't feel the normal range of human emotions. Therefore, anything that makes their persona more realistic is pleasurable to the narcissist. Because they are so empty, they can lie effortlessly. They can look people in the eye and lie without feeling any remorse. Narcissists lie like children. You can catch a child with chocolate around her mouth, you'll ask if she ate the chocolate, and she'll shake her head in denial. But a narcissist will give you a well-thought-out story in an attempt to convince you they're telling the truth. They enjoy exploiting people and take advantage of the natural desire some people have to help others. The narcissist will create a range of problems, ailments, and injuries to get people to feel sorry for him. Common scenarios they will make up for pity include car accidents, crazy exes, someone defrauded them of their money, and fake illnesses.

People lie on a spectrum; most of us tell a white lie every now and then. But narcissists don't tell white lies. They are pathological chronic liars. They are unscrupulous, deceitful, manipulative, and deceptive. The narcissist lies to tap into the victim's insecurities. They start out lying about themselves, their accomplishments, how much money they make, the terrible relationship they've just come out of, and they lie about how they feel about you. They will lie about you when you're in the relationship, and at the end of the relationship, they'll lie to everyone about you being the crazy ex-partner. Then they'll lie about the lies they've told! You will never hear the truth from a narcissist. If their lips are moving, they're lying!

Listen, it's real easy to become a victim of narcissistic abuse because, as you've read, they start out as your Prince Charming, and then they turn into Jekyll and

Hyde. But there are other reasons why you ended up in a relationship with a narcissist, and we'll get into that next.

Chapter 3: Why am I a Narcissist Magnet?

"You must tell yourself, no matter how hard it is, or how hard it gets, I'm going to make it." ~ Les Brown

I jumped from one narcissistic relationship to the next until I learned why I kept attracting this type of man. Don't worry, there's nothing fundamentally wrong with you. Unfortunately, the problem is that you're *too* nice. The bad news is that until you break away from your limiting subconscious beliefs, you'll keep attracting narcissists because it's an addiction. But before we get into that, let's take a look at why you're a narcissist magnet.

You Were Raised in a Narcissistic Household:
Imagine a father who intentionally makes his children feel confused by telling them they're imagining things when they try and explain something they've experienced? Or a mother who acts like the kind, doting parent in public, but as soon as they get home, screams and rages at her children and husband when they do something to upset her. Parents with narcissistic traits treat their children this way.

When children are raised by narcissistic parents, they grow up believing they are deficient or inferior in some way. In general, narcissistic parents are overwhelmingly close to their children. Their kids are an extension of their perceived excellence, and they become a source of unhealthy pride for the parent. "Didn't I do such a fabulous job? Look at how wonderful my children are." They use their children as a source of supply. People praise the parents because of how great their kids are.

The children learn to conform to their parents' standards. Any part of them that's considered unacceptable is shut down. This causes anxiety in the child because they know that the only way to please their parents is if they act in a certain way. Narcissistic parents make their children's lives very difficult if they reject their agenda. They are not allowed to have thoughts or feelings of their own, and if they do, it leads to punishment. As a result, the child learns that their thoughts and feelings are invalid and unimportant, and they will suppress how they really feel to avoid conflict in the home.

As you are aware, narcissists can be really nice, but this kindness doesn't come without a price. The children will eventually understand that their relationship is based on give and take. "Whatever I do for you, you've got to repay me somehow." So even acts of kindness become a source of contention to the children raised in households with narcissistic parents. For an adult, narcissistic behavior is difficult to deal with, but for children, it's absolute torture. Their unpredictable nature is extremely unsettling, and a child can't get up and leave the house; they're trapped in that environment until they're old enough to move out. The child starts believing that they're the problem. *If I was good at football, my dad would love me.* Or *If I was pretty enough to enter a pageant, my mom would be proud of me.* The parents' false ideology that they're the perfect parent reinforces the child's belief that they are not good enough, and that's the only reason why they get into trouble.

The problem with growing up in a narcissistic household is the child thinks their experiences are normal. They don't know anything else because that's the environment they've been raised in since birth, and children become products of their environments. Experts say that men marry women like their mothers, and women marry men like their fathers. Without getting too scientific here, that's because we are driven by our subconscious minds. You can compare the subconscious mind to a computer hard drive. No one sees it, but it's the most important part of the computer. The hard drive is where all the information is stored. Even if your computer breaks down, an expert can access the hard drive and extract what you need. The mind is the same. It's divided into two parts. The conscious mind is where all our thinking and reasoning takes place. But the subconscious mind is where everything we have seen, heard, and experienced since conception is stored. Research suggests that by the age of 18, we have the equivalent of 100 encyclopedias worth of information stored in the subconscious mind. And that includes every word our parents have ever spoken to us. The subconscious mind is more powerful than we could ever imagine, but the problem is that the information stored in it is what drives us. And if you were raised in an abusive household, your subconscious mind will lead you into abusive situations because that's all it knows. If you were raised by narcissistic parents, that's why you attract narcissistic partners.

You're an Empath: The term opposites attract has never been truer than when describing empaths and narcissists. Narcissists are attracted to people they can get the most supply from. For this reason, they often target empaths. Empaths, on the other hand, tune in to the emotions of others and feel them as if they were their own. They are emotional sponges and hate suffering, and have a deep desire to make the world a better place. For this reason, narcissists are extremely attracted to them because they see them as selfless people who will go to great lengths to fulfill their needs.

Author of *The Empath's Survival Guide,* Judith Orloff, states that the narcissist/empath relationship is a toxic one that always ends in disaster. During the love-bombing stage, empaths are drawn to the kind and giving version of the narcissist. They are completely oblivious to the evil that awaits behind the mask. Orloff argues that empaths should never fall in love with narcissists, but this violates their instincts because once the narcissist's true colors start to show, the empath feels bound to helping them. Empaths find it difficult to accept that it's impossible to heal a person with their love.

The empath's goal is harmony, while the narcissist's is chaos and drama. They take pleasure in knowing they can trigger negative reactions in people. Narcissists string empaths along with their manipulation tactics, giving them hope every so often that one day, things will be better. Empaths are very understanding because they know that humans are flawed and imperfect beings. For this reason, they are willing to be patient through someone's struggles. If the narcissist says, "I know I've made mistakes in this relationship, but that's because I'm not perfect, and I know I need to change. Can you help me?" That's all an empath needs to hear to give the narcissist another chance. I'm an empath, and Steve said this to me countless times throughout our relationship, and surprise, surprise, he never changed. It's nothing but a manipulation tactic the narcissist uses to reel his victim back in, and it worked on me for many years.

You Have Low Self-Esteem: People with low self-esteem and narcissists have a magnetic attraction to each other. A person with low self-esteem is easy to spot because they typically wear their heart on their sleeve and will give you massive clues that they're insecure. For example, when you pay them a compliment, instead of saying thank you, they respond with something like, "I don't know what you see in me." A response like this is basically a green light to a narcissist. In their mind, they've found a potential victim.

Don't take this the wrong way, but insecure people and narcissists are similar in two very distinct aspects. They both need supply to validate their sense of self, and their partners are the only people who get to see who they really are. What do I mean by this? The person with low self-esteem doesn't value themselves, and they seek out people who are going to validate them. You will find that insecure people are always in a relationship because, in their flawed state, they can't give themselves what they need. They believe they are worthless, and that's the voice they tune in to when they are single. But when they find a partner who tells them how attractive, special, and awesome they are, it drowns out their own negative self-talk and makes them feel good about themselves, and they get hooked on that. The narcissist does this very well during the love-bombing stage, but then the insecure person starts living out their worst nightmare when the abuse arrives. Insults such as ugly, stupid, no one will ever love you, etc., cut like a knife because these words are confirming how they truly feel about themselves.

Your Love is Unconditional: We all use our cell phones a lot—in fact, most of us can't live without them—and when they're not working, we miss them and realize how much value it actually adds to our lives. Narcissistic "love" is the same. Bear with me, I'm going somewhere with this.

Okay, so, you know when you really love someone, they can make you really angry, but despite how you feel, the love you have for them is still there? That's what is meant by unconditional love, and narcissists have no concept of this. Healthy unconditional love requires a connection that's more than just skin deep. It's not about appearance or what someone does for you. It's a bond that connects your very core; your souls are intertwined. This doesn't mean you don't have limits, and you'll tolerate anything. You might get to a point where the relationship is no longer sustainable because the way they treat you is unacceptable, but to some degree, you still have love for them.

Narcissistic love is totally superficial. We love our cell phones until they stop working, then it's a "piece of crap." Who decides what a cell phone does? We do. We control who we want it to call, what we want it to find online, what we want it to take pictures of, etc. In the same way, narcissists decide what the people in their lives are supposed to do, and when those demands are not met, the scene can become a lot like what happens when the cell phone no longer works, and we start swearing at it and calling it every name under the sun. I've been there, so I know what I'm talking about! It's not a love based on a deep soul tie, it's all about functionality. When my phone stops working, and I've got to replace it, I don't shed a tear. I just go and replace it. I might be aggravated about the money I've got to spend, but other than that, it's sayonara, out with the old and in with the new.

Unconditional love isn't about appearances. It's about being aware of the presence of another soul. For a narcissist, it would be like asking them to sit in front of a TV screen and asking that they connect to its soul. Sounds strange, right? Because a television doesn't have a soul, so there isn't going to be anything to connect with. What am I trying to tell you? That some people can't see beyond the superficial image of the person standing in front of them. It might come naturally to you, but some people don't have that capacity. A person who can't connect with their own soul won't be able to connect with someone else's soul.

It's impossible to understand a narcissist from the perspective of unconditional love; it's terribly confusing. I compare it to a flower with unlimited petals. Remember those days sitting under the bright summer sky playing, "he loves me, he loves me not," hoping that fate will give you the answers you're looking for regarding your love interest? Although that uncertainty was gut-wrenching, when you were in love with a normal person, eventually, you'd get an answer. But not with a narcissist because they don't know what unconditional love is. They love you when they think your behavior is acceptable, and if it's not, that love is withdrawn. Ask a narcissist if they love someone, and they'll say they do, but what they really mean is, "Yes, I love him like my cell phone, as long as he's working the way I want him to."

In short, narcissists are attracted to people who love unconditionally because whether the narcissist is defective or not, their partner is going to love them regardless. They are not going to replace the narcissist like they would a cell phone. They'll keep trying to fix the relationship by loving the narcissist deeper and harder, but once you reach burnout and your supply dries up, the narcissist will discard you like a broken cell phone.

Well, now that you know why you're a narcissist magnet, it's time to get out of the relationship and stay out! But it's a complicated process. In Chapter 4, I'll provide you with the most effective strategies to get out of a relationship with a narcissist.

Chapter 4: How to End a Relationship with a Narcissist

"Walking away from someone you love is not an immoral thing." ~ Arien Smith

Now, this is where it gets difficult because narcissists don't take too well to being dumped. In their world, they do the rejecting and not you. The reality is that no one likes being rejected. It can make us feel insecure, depressed, and sometimes angry. But the difference between a narcissist and the average person is that they will take advantage of the rejection and see it as constructive criticism. They will use it to better themselves in the area they were rejected. Let's say a relationship ends because one party felt that the other was lacking in communication skills, which made it difficult to have a conversation with them and resolve conflict in a way that will improve their union. As painful as that might be to hear, the recipient will think, *Okay, I'm going to learn as much as I can about communication skills, so I won't have this problem in my next relationship.* Accepting criticism is a form of self-reflection, and as you've read, narcissists don't have the capacity to do this, which is why rejection is so difficult for them to handle.

Remember, the narcissist operates from a false sense of self. She lives in a fictitious world she has made up in her head. She has spent a lifetime constructing an image that she is this perfect and superior being. She expects everyone to love her for the person she portrays herself to be. If people are not worshipping the ground that the narcissist walks on, it terrifies her. Her immediate assumption is that they can see through the act, that they have seen into the deep crevices of her soul and discovered that she's not who she says she is but a weak, pathetic individual who detests the very fibers of her own being. This is why a narcissist can't look within, because they are forced to face who they really are. And that's the reason why you can't dump a narcissist and expect to continue living a normal life afterward. By ending a relationship with a narcissist, you are essentially saying, "I can see straight through your mask. I know who you really are." The narcissist has invested too much time and energy into her fake persona for someone to blow her cover, and by any means necessary, she will make sure it doesn't happen. So let me start by telling you what you can expect when you take steps to end your relationship with a narcissist.

Narcissistic Rage

You may have been subjected to narcissistic rage several times during your relationship, and leaving your partner may trigger it. Narcissistic rage is when their overgrown ego or grandiose sense of self-worth is downplayed. This is caused by a "narcissistic scar" or a "narcissistic injury." As a result, they are subjected to emotional pain, their reaction is intense, and the situation can go from zero to one hundred real quick. Narcissistic rage is dangerous because they can't control it. Psychologically, it's how they protect themselves from the perceived shame they are unwilling to confront. It's important to mention that narcissistic rage is not the same as anger. Yes, anger can get out of control, but rage is on another level.

Narcissistic rage is triggered by issues that wouldn't have an effect on the average person. A denial or disagreement of any sort, no matter how small, can catapult a narcissist into a severe rage. Once they sense feelings of shame, they suppress those feelings with narcissistic rage. For everyone else, anger is processed through seven levels of emotion. Although they may vary from person to person, according to psychologists, they include the following:

- **Stress:** Anger is first felt on a subconscious level before it is expressed.
- **Anxiety:** A subtle way of expressing anger.
- **Agitation:** Openly expressing displeasure without blame.

- **Irritation:** Letting someone know you are unhappy in an attempt to get a reaction.
- **Frustration:** Harsh words or a change in facial expression to show anger.
- **Anger:** Vocalizing anger by shouting as well as dramatic body movements.
- **Rage:** Complete loss of and inability to control temper

Narcissists don't follow this path; they go from stress to rage without processing the information that has led to their feelings of anger. In their mind, their rage is acceptable. To a normal person, it's irrational.

The Causes of Narcissistic Rage: As mentioned, narcissistic rage is caused by narcissistic injury or narcissistic scarring, which are triggered by the following:

- **Injury to Self-Esteem:** When a narcissistic person's self-esteem has been attacked, it triggers feelings of failure or shame. Because narcissists believe they are superior beings that deserve special treatment, if any of their weaknesses are pointed out, even in a constructive way, their reaction is intense anger. As far as the narcissist is concerned, they're being attacked, and their response is to get revenge on the accuser. Sometimes this can result in violence.

- **Challenge to Confidence:** A narcissist must appear confident and self-assured at all times. It's usually the people closest to them who challenge their confidence because that's who they spend the most time with. Let's say you and your boyfriend are having a conversation about history, he gets a date wrong, and you correct him. He won't thank you for giving him the right information. He'll see it as an assault on his superior intelligence, which challenges his confidence. To protect his ego or to overpower you, he'll have an outburst.

- **A Challenge to False Sense of Self:** You can't get away with doubting a narcissist because it presents a challenge to their false sense of self. As his partner, you've been his main source of supply, and you've nurtured this false sense of self for a long time. He is used to you lavishing him with praise and adoration. The minute you doubt anything he says or does, the fear is that you can now see them how they truly see themselves: unlovable and unworthy.

Types of Narcissistic Rage: There are two types of narcissistic rage: passive-aggressive and explosive:

- **Passive-Aggressive:** This is a more subtle type of narcissistic rage that involves punishing the victim by withdrawing all forms of communication. They might pull a disappearing act, stop talking to you, or refuse to respond to phone calls and text messages.

- **Explosive:** Again, this is one of the main reasons why you should absolutely, categorically not tell your narcissistic partner you want out of the relationship! You will activate all three forms of narcissistic injury at once, and you are at risk of getting physically hurt. This is especially true if you're dealing with a high-spectrum malignant narcissist. Explosive narcissistic rage can manifest in the form of screaming and yelling, destroying property, and excessive violence.

The Hoovering Strategy

Let's say you make the mistake of letting the narcissist know you're leaving and they still have access to you. He will wait a while and let everything simmer down, but as if he's got an antenna that lets him know when to strike, you'll get a message out of the blue. And it will literally be when you're down in the dumps. It will say something like, *You were amazing.* You'll get an immediate dopamine hit, coupled with that sinking feeling in the pit of your stomach telling you that maybe, just maybe, things could work out between you. This is what psychologists have termed "hoovering." Think of the involuntary sucking motion of a hoover; that's what the narcissist is doing to you. It's a manipulation tactic the narcissist uses to pull you back into his world, and more often than not, it works. Here are some of the most common signs of hoovering:

Random Messaging: As mentioned, sending you a random message is the narcissist's way of trying to reel you back into the relationship. Be on guard for seemingly benign questions or messages of nostalgia. He doesn't care about the answer; the aim is to get you thinking about him again. Here are some examples:

- "I had a dream about you."
- "Have you still got my blue t-shirt?"
- "I'm listening to our song, thinking about the way things used to be."

Important Dates: Making contact on your birthday or during the holidays is a tactic to get you to answer their phone calls or texts. If they find out through the grapevine that you've got a promotion, you might get a message congratulating you on your new position. He couldn't give a toss about your promotion; his aim is to get you to think that he actually cares about your well-being so that you lower your guard.

They've Changed: This is the one time you'll hear a narcissist admitting their mistakes, but it's for one reason and one reason only, so don't fall for it! He will call you crying and apologizing for all the wrong he did in the relationship. For the times he made you cry and feel insecure. He might even go as far as sending you a voice note or video message of him crying and telling you how sorry he is.

Declaring His Undying Love: The narcissist will revert back to the love-bombing stage because he knows that's one strategy that definitely works. He will revert back to all the sweet nothings he whispered in your ear when he was getting you hooked and message you with things like:

- "No one else will ever be able to make me feel like you do."
- "We belong together. You're my soul mate."
- "You were perfect. No one else will do."

Bombarding You with Gifts: And I mean BOMBARDING! When Steve first left me high and dry and just disappeared out of the blue, he began his hoovering campaign by sending me gifts several times a day. He knew I loved surprises, and he also knew what type of presents I liked. So he just kept sending them to me; he sent them to my job, my home. He even went as far as to send presents to my gym because he knew what time I started and finished my workouts! This went on for one full month, and he probably spent thousands of dollars, but it worked. I got sucked right back into his web of deceit and started thinking about getting back with him.

Unrealistic Promises: When you first started dating your partner, he promised you the world. He was going to marry you and give you three children, buy you a mansion, and give you the life of your dreams. During the devaluing stage of your relationship, he conveniently forgot that he had made any of those promises. He might have said something like, "There is no way I said I'd marry you and give you three children because first of all, I don't want to get married, and second of all, I hate kids. So why would I say something like that?" Don't let your mind play tricks on you. If he starts making these promises again, it's not because he means it. It's because he knows they got you hooked last time, so he's using the same strategy.

Using Other People: Be on the lookout for hoover by proxy. This happens when he takes on the victim role and gets in contact with everyone you know, acting as if he's been so hard done by. He will do things like:

- Contact your parents and talk about how much he misses you and that he doesn't understand why you've just abandoned the relationship like this. Meanwhile, he's the one who dumped you!

- Telling your mutual friends that he made a massive mistake ending the relationship, and he desperately wants to get back with you.
- Using your child as a pawn in his game by getting them to give you messages.

The narcissist will use other people in this way, hoping that your loved ones will be able to speak some sense into you and convince you to get back with him.

They Need Help: The narcissist will make up a grandiose story in an attempt to pull on your heartstrings. For me, this is where it crosses the line. Steve went as far as to tell me he had cancer...pick your jaw up off the floor, no word of a lie! After bombarding me with gifts, he knew he had nearly got me, so he waited a couple of weeks and sent me a picture of him lying in a hospital bed, along with some official-looking hospital documents stating that he had stage 3 bowel cancer! The reason why he was sending me all those gifts was because he didn't have much time left, and since he didn't have any children, he wanted to spend all his money on the person he loved the most...me. I fell for it hook, line, and sinker and immediately allowed him to move back in. Well, surprise, surprise, he wouldn't allow me to attend doctor appointments with him. His excuse was that it was so traumatic, and he didn't want me to see him like that. When I started asking about chemotherapy, he said he was starting it in two weeks' time. When he returned home after his imaginary doctor's appointment, the cancer had miraculously disappeared. The doctors were amazed; they had never seen anything like it. He was completely healed! The joke is that I believed him. We even went on vacation to celebrate his victory! Guess how I found out he was lying? During the discard phase when he decided to leave me again. During one of his rants, he let me know that I was terribly stupid and naïve for believing that he had cancer because it was a lie to get me to come back to him, and it worked. He then burst into the most demonic-sounding cackle I've ever heard.

Spreading Rumors: When it comes to hoovering, this is often the last resort for the narcissist. He will either make up the rumors himself and spread them amongst friends and family members, or he will send you messages saying that he's heard people talking about you. Don't take the bait. This is just a desperate attempt to get your attention. He hopes you'll call him wanting to find out more about what's been said. The reality is that no one has said anything. Every false story circulating about you was made up by him.

Making Ridiculous Accusations: After excessively trying to contact you by phone, text message, and email, and you don't respond, the narcissist will start accusing you of things. For example, he'll message you and claim that he saw you on a date with one of his friends or that one of his coworkers said they saw you out the other day and you are fully pregnant. Again, the aim is to get your defenses up so you respond.

Playing Dumb: This one will cause you to fall out flat on your back in disbelief! About a month after Steve had left me with no furniture in my apartment, he showed up at my job and asked for a ride home because he'd caught a flat. My first reaction was shock. I hadn't seen or heard from this guy in over a month, and he turns up at my work asking for a ride home! What on Earth was going on? He then stated, "Yeah, I need you to drop me back to our apartment so I can pick up my tennis equipment, then to the tennis courts, because me and Dave have a match at 7:00 p.m. Come on. Quickly! Time is of the essence." I was standing there like, wait a minute, hold on, are you kidding me right now? He was basically acting as if nothing had happened. He hadn't left, we were still together, and everything was just fine. That didn't work. At this point, I just thought he was crazy! I later learned that playing dumb was one of the many hoovering tactics used by narcissists. This strategy also involves turning up at important events as if you gave them a personal invitation. For example, he may know that you take your mother to a certain restaurant for her birthday every year.

Threatening to Self-Harm: One of the most common hoovering tactics is threatening to self-harm if you don't respond to their texts, phone calls, or emails. They may even go as far as stating they are going to commit suicide. I do not take self-harm or suicide lightly, and if you believe your ex-partner is in any immediate danger, call the police. However, it's also important to understand that a person who is serious about self-harm or suicide isn't going to announce it to the world; they'll just do it. So don't fall for this manipulation tactic.

Save Some Money: Unless you've got a stack of cash ready and waiting for your escape, you'll need to save some money. If you can get a loan or a raise on your credit card, then do so because your aim should be to get out as quickly as possible. This is literally going to be the great escape. As you will read shortly, the narcissist won't let you go without a fight. If you've got a job, you'll need to hand in your notice. If your partner lives in your house, you'll need to leave. Unless you've got some friends and relatives that he doesn't know about, you'll need to rent somewhere to stay because trust and do believe, he's going to come looking for you. When you get to where you're going, you don't know how long it will take before you get another job, so make sure you've got enough cash before you make your exit.

Report the Abuse: Unless you feel that your life is in danger, there's no need to report the abuse to the police.

However, you do need to let friends and family know. As you've probably experienced, narcissists isolate you. I was with Steve for ten years, and I can count on one hand the number of times I saw my family and friends during that time. Any time there was a family get-together or a social event, I made excuses as to why I couldn't attend. No one suspected a thing because Steve made sure that he moved us to another state, so it literally made it impossible for me to make it anyway. My family assumed I had found my happy ever after with the man of my dreams. Little did they know I was living a real-life nightmare.

When I decided to leave, I used a friend's phone at work to call my dad. I told him all about it. My father and my brother jumped on the first flight to Chicago and brought me back home. Steve hunted me down like a dog. I literally had to go into hiding for a year. Every weekend, he was in Chicago, knocking on my parents' door and turning up at friends' houses. I eventually got a restraining order against him because his behavior got really weird. This is why you've got to tell your friends and family about the abuse; first, if they don't know, they're likely to innocently tell him where you are, and second, you need the support network. Getting out of an abusive relationship is really hard, and you're going to need all the help you can get.

No More Chances: According to Dr. Perpetua Neo, the founder of Detox Your Heart, an abuse victim will return to the relationship seven times before they find the courage to leave for good. What I mean by no more chances is that once you've made up your mind, leave. After reading the first four chapters of this book, you know full well that your partner is a narcissist, and it's time to go. Don't try and justify his behavior in your head, or convince yourself that if you play your cards right, he'll change. He is not going to change. I don't know where on the NPD spectrum your partner is, but if he's on the high end, things could get dangerous, which is why you need to get out now!

Log Out of All Devices: If you've used any of your partner's devices and your details have been saved, he can track you. Make a list of all the sites you know your details are saved on autofill, and any time you get the chance, start deleting them. There are some apps or websites that will allow you to save all your passwords; create a security boundary by doing a master reset. If your partner has a habit of confiscating your phones, get a cheap replacement.

Undercover Exit: The most stupid thing you can do is to tell a narcissist you're leaving them. They are not like normal people. He won't just get upset and want to know why you're leaving him. He'll pull out every weapon in his arsenal to get you to stay. He will revert to love-bombing you, flattery, and professing his undying, unfailing, and everlasting love for you. He'll cuss you out and declare you'll never find another lover like him. Hell, he might even hold you hostage depending on how crazy he is.

The one and only reason why a narcissist will want you to stay after you tell them you're ending the relationship is because, in their world, that's not how it goes. He does the discarding, not you. He will want you to stay so that he can work his magic, get you hooked again, and then dump you in the most vile and cruel way. I don't know your individual circumstances, so I can't advise you on the best way to make your exit. All I can say is that he absolutely, categorically doesn't need to know about it.

Photocopy Your Documents: This is really important if you're from a different country and the best way for you to escape is to go home. If your partner catches wind that you're about to leave, it's not uncommon for the narcissist to destroy your documents to prevent you from escaping. Take a photocopy of your documents and send them to your email. Preferably, a dummy account he knows nothing about. Do the same with any other official documents such as your birth certificate, driving license, and bank details.

No Contact: Once you've left, don't go back. In a normal relationship, one or both parties want closure when it ends, and they might meet up to discuss it. Not so with a narcissist. He will not admit that he's played a role in the breakdown of your relationship. You will get zero answers about what went wrong, so don't even bother to try. Additionally, you've made all this effort to leave, so is there really any point in turning back? This is what no physical contact should look like:

- No social media following
- No direct messages on social media
- No phone calls
- No text messages
- No accepting gifts
- No staying friends
- No hanging out with mutual friends
- No casual hookups
- No meetups

This is what no emotional or spiritual contact should look like:

- No keeping gifts they bought you
- No planning how to get revenge
- No going over painful memories
- No having conversations in your head with the narcissist
- No justifying the narcissist's behavior in your head
- No watching movies/listening to music that reminds you of the narcissist

- No driving to places that remind you of the narcissist
- No looking at photos of you and the narcissist together
- No thinking about the good old days

Now that you've left the relationship and you are in a place of safety, it's time to start healing, and the first and most difficult step is to process the trauma you've just experienced.

Chapter 5: Processing Your Trauma

"Trauma is a fact of life. It does not, however, have to be a life sentence."

~ Peter A. Levine

Psychological trauma is not something you should underestimate. When it comes to processing your trauma, your first point of contact should be with a psychologist. I had to go through years of therapy to become who I am today, and all the tips I am about to provide came from a trained psychologist. They worked for me, so I can only assume they will work for you. But before I begin, I want you to get a full understanding of trauma, and I'll start with physical trauma:

Physical Trauma: Trauma to the body involves wounds which might include broken bones, damage to the internal organs, gunshot wounds, or stab wounds. Physical trauma is broken down into two categories:

- **Blunt Trauma:** Injuries of this nature are inflicted with a blunt instrument to the outside of the body. This includes burns, punches, kicks, crush injuries, injuries from a road traffic accident.

- **Penetrating Trauma:** Injuries of this nature are inflicted by a sharp object, and they penetrate the body. This includes stabbing, shooting, or falling onto a sharp object.

Physical trauma is either minor or major; a minor injury such as a cut finger or a stubbed toe is uncomfortable, but in most cases, the injury is treated at home. A serious injury will require hospital admission for evaluation, treatment, and rehabilitation. When the patient first arrives at the hospital, how badly a person has been injured is not always apparent and will require an examination by a scan or an x-ray. A scoring system is used to calculate the severity of the injury; it is known as the Injury Severity Score (ISS). Once all the injuries have been diagnosed, the score is calculated retrospectively. Some hospitals are dedicated to treating specific types of trauma.

Psychological Trauma: Unfortunately, there is very little awareness about psychological trauma, and for this reason, it is often left untreated and can cause long-lasting emotional damage. But in the same way physical trauma affects the body and requires treatment, so does psychological trauma affect the brain and require treatment. Think about it like this. If you got stabbed, why would you just sit there and bleed out? You're going to call an ambulance, go to the hospital, and get treated. If you left it, one of two things is going to happen: you are either going to bleed to death, or you'll get an infection that will eventually kill you. Psychological trauma can occur because of:

- Events or situations we find traumatic
- Experiences that affect us

Psychological trauma can happen at any age, and everyone reacts differently to it. In most cases, you won't know you've experienced psychological trauma unless you are professionally diagnosed. Additionally, symptoms of trauma may not manifest until years after the experience.

Experiences That Cause Trauma: Trauma is personal. Two people can go through exactly the same experience, and one person ends up chronically depressed, the other one doesn't. Trauma is typically caused when you are made to feel:

- Powerless
- Ashamed
- Trapped
- Unsupported
- Unsafe
- Invalidated
- Abandoned
- Rejected
- Humiliated

- Under threat
- Frightened

Trauma can happen because of the following:

- Living in a traumatic environment
- Seeing someone else get harmed
- Direct harm caused to yourself
- Ongoing or one-off events
- Treatment by family or community

Trauma can lead to mental health problems such as post-traumatic stress disorder, depression, and anxiety, which is why you should start working on your recovery immediately. Here are some tips to get you started:

Recovery is a Process: Please understand that dating a narcissist is the equivalent of walking through hell and just managing to escape alive. Your brain and your nervous system have been hammered. In the same way, you're not just going to start walking on a broken leg after an accident, your mind isn't going to snap back into place because you've left the relationship. As mentioned, the recovery process for psychological trauma is no different than the steps you would take for physical trauma. Using the broken leg example, once the injury has been examined and the extent of the damage has been determined, you will either need surgery or your leg is placed in a calf straight away. The doctors will instruct you not to walk on the leg until it is almost fully healed. You may need to do some light exercises just to keep the blood flowing. When the doctor determines that you can start walking on it again, you are given crutches and referred to a physiotherapist. Only once your leg has fully healed will you be able to walk, run, and jump on it again.

It is also important to mention that the healing process is your responsibility. Unfortunately, there is no magic pill I can give you to take the pain away and restore your sanity. The person with a broken leg won't heal if they don't put the work in. But it's going to take a while before you get better. I can't tell you how long your healing journey will take because everyone is different. Unlike physical healing, psychological healing is a lifelong process. You are never fully healed; all it takes is a momentary mental lapse, and you're right back where you started. Therefore, you've got to turn your recovery process into a lifestyle and incorporate the most helpful strategies into your daily routine.

Ask for Support: I had a really difficult time asking for help after I left Steve. First and foremost, I had abandoned my friends and family to marry this guy, and I really felt ashamed that I needed them now. In my head, I thought they were just being polite and didn't really want anything to do with me. After all, I'm the one who disappeared. How dare I expect them to help me now? My anxiety got the better of me for a while until I came to my senses and realized that people actually wanted to help me. I had lost a few friends, and I totally understood. They had moved on in life, and my situation wasn't something they really wanted to get involved with. But in general, everyone was really loving and supportive. Friends I hadn't seen in years went above and beyond the call of duty to make sure I had everything I needed.

Nevertheless, in general, people find it difficult to ask for help because they're hardwired to be independent. According to psychologist Dr. Rosie Mae, asking for help makes people feel uncomfortable because they're handing over their control to another person. Anyone who has just come out of an abusive relationship will struggle because this is what they were forced to do. Their abuser had full control over their life, and the thought of giving it away again terrifies them. Additionally, people don't like being perceived as needy. We don't want to seem incompetent, so we work extra hard to ensure we are not seen in this way. There is also the tendency to think that everyone's got their own problems to deal with, so why do they want to add your issues to the equation? Some people also fear they'll be rejected or shunned if they ask for help. But as I found, the irony is that people do want to help. It's human nature to want to help others. The good news is that you can get better at asking for help. Here are a few tips:

- **You Are Not Weak:** Changing the way you view asking for help will make it a lot easier for you to reach out to people when you need it. Asking for help and having a strong support network isn't a weakness, it's a strength. Since hearing it wasn't enough to convince me, my therapist told me about all the successful people like Warren Buffet and Richard Branson who all have support networks. Athletes might have the talent, but they need coaches to push them into greatness. They point out their blind spots and get them to focus on their strengths. The athlete focuses on the training routine provided by the coach that will eventually lead to a successful outcome. By asking for help, you are refusing to allow external circumstances to hold you back and are taking control of your life. Accepting your weakness is courageous.

- **Reframe:** Sometimes, asking for help can sound transactional because of the way we ask. Calling a friend and saying, "Can you look after my kids while I go and see my therapist? I'll return the favor." For one, you are assuming that your friend will only help you if you help him/her. Second, you've now put pressure on yourself to fulfill an obligation that you might not be able to. You can prevent this by reframing your request and turn it into a conversation instead of a transaction. You could say something like, "I've got a challenge, and I would appreciate your help. Let's have a chat about it and see what we can come up with." Instead of directly asking your friend to look after your kids while you go to your appointment, they may be able to give you some practical advice on services that help parents with childcare for hospital appointments. Or they might know someone who provides cheap childcare. In this way, you're covered for the next time you need a babysitter. Additionally, you are being more respectful to your friend and developing a deeper connection with them at the same time.

- **Be Honest:** People are not mind readers. Your loved ones are not going to know you need help or emotional support if you don't ask for it. Victims of narcissistic abuse have a habit of isolating themselves because they don't want to risk becoming vulnerable again. To the abuse victim, being vulnerable feels like you are giving away your power. It triggers the same fear you experienced in your relationship. However, you've got to keep reminding yourself that you're safe now. You are surrounded by people who genuinely love and care about you.

Don't Suppress Your Feelings

Let me warn you now: You are going to feel terrible after you leave your relationship. In fact, you'll feel worse than when you were in it. You'll feel abandoned, betrayed, lonely, like a fool for allowing the abuse to happen, depressed, and every other negative emotion you can think of. You will experience a tidal wave of intense emotions, so debilitating that sometimes, you'll feel paralyzed. About a week after I broke up with Steve, I was in so much emotional pain that I sat and stared at a wall for 48 hours! It was terrible. I didn't know what to do with myself. A lot of people go back to their abusive relationship at this point because it feels better. It makes no sense, and the only way I can describe it is that it's like an addict going cold turkey. They know the drug is killing them, but the withdrawal symptoms from not having the drug in their system feels worse than taking the drugs they know could end their life. Some addicts get through the cold turkey phase, and others don't.

The Consequences of Emotional Suppression

Whether you are going through physical or emotional healing, it gets worse before it gets better, and it's essential that you push through the pain because, on the other side, there's freedom. When emotional trauma is so intense, you don't want to deal with it, so you suppress your emotions and act as if they don't exist. When I was dealing with the breakup with Steve, numbing out was what I did best. As soon as my feelings showed up, I'd pick up a glass of wine, go to bed, or watch a movie. Whatever sheltered me from the storm of hurt, guilt, anger, loneliness, anxiety, and depression is what I ran to. It's an emotional regulation strategy that has a lot of negative consequences.

The Rebound Effect: A study conducted in 1987 involved one group of participants being asked to ignore thoughts about a white bear. The second group was allowed to think about a white bear and anything else that came to their mind. The group that was told to suppress their feelings of a white bear had more thoughts about the white bear than the participants who were allowed to let their thoughts roam. Experts have labeled the results of this study the "rebound effect."

Trying to avoid your negative emotions sets a vicious cycle in motion, the more you refuse to confront your feelings, the more negative feelings you'll experience. Studies have found that emotional suppression is the reason why people who suffer from conditions such as obsessive-compulsive disorder, post-traumatic stress disorder, and bipolar disorder are bombarded with painful emotions.

Premature Death: A study conducted by the Harvard School of Public Health found that emotional suppression increases the risk of early death by more than 30 percent.

Increased Risk of Cancer: In 2013, the University of Rochester and the Harvard School of Public Health conducted a study that found people who didn't deal with their emotions increased their risk of a cancer diagnosis by 70 percent.

A Negative Outlook: When you suppress emotions such as anger and sadness, you put a limit on the various emotions you can feel. This includes positive emotions such as happiness and joy. In other words, if you are not experiencing positive emotions, you're stuck in a negative frame of mind.

Weight Gain: I can most definitely attest to this one because binge eating made me feel better. It gave me the greatest joy to order ridiculous amounts of fast food and snacks, sit in front of the TV, and stuff my face for hours. Unhealthy food became my temporary Band-Aid. One of the strange benefits of weight gain for some people is that it acts as a reminder that they need to deal with their problems. I remember looking in the mirror one day and being disgusted with myself because of the amount of weight I'd put on. It was at that moment that I told myself, "No more!" I need to get my life together, and I haven't looked back since.

Migraines and Headaches: One way the body reacts to emotional stress is that the muscles in your brow and forehead tighten. This restricts blood flow to the brain, which causes headaches.

Stomach Problems: Research conducted by the Harvard Medical School found that stress from repressed emotions leads to ulcers, vomiting, bloating, gas, and slow digestion.

Mental Exhaustion: When you suppress your emotions, you are also suppressing the memory of the event that hurt you. However, the mind won't allow you to forget, so your brain has got to work overtime to keep pushing the memory out.

How to Regulate Your Emotions

According to psychologist Caroline Fenkel, while you're exhausting your energy hiding from your feelings, those emotions are in another room doing strength training exercises. When you're done binge eating, drinking, sitting in front of the TV, or whatever else you were doing to suppress your feelings, you feel ten times worse, and you wonder why. It's because your feelings were lifting weights in the other room. So what's the alternative? The answer is to deal with your emotions in a healthy way. Here are some tips on emotional regulation:

What Does Numbing Look Like to You: "Know thy self" are three very important words. You've got to know what you're fighting against before you can beat it. And sometimes, we don't even realize we are participating in destructive behaviors until we experience the consequences. Therefore, take some time out to think about the things you do to numb your emotions. Sometimes it's a form of distraction, entertainment, or food, drugs, and alcohol. But some are a bit more subtle, like busyness, working overtime, and making sure you've got so much to do that you don't have time to think about your emotions. Another tactic people use to handle feelings they don't want to deal with is becoming a gossip and constantly putting their nose into other people's business. Or becoming the self-help guru of your social circle and always being there for your friends and family giving them advice that you yourself don't implement.

Identify Your Feelings: Most of us don't evaluate our emotions when we feel them. We either react or ignore them. The body is designed to experience emotions, and we can't experience what we're not aware of. You will feel your emotions in your body. They might manifest as tightness in your throat, a buzzing sound in your head, your heart beating in your chest, or a feeling in your gut. The next step is to think about what triggered the emotion; it might be something that's easy to identify, such as a newspaper article about domestic violence. Or it might be something you need to think about a bit more deeply, such as a picture of your friend's wedding on Instagram. Ordinarily, this should trigger positive emotions. Your friend has just gotten married to the man of her dreams, and she's happy; you can see it in the pictures. However, you're not upset that your friend got married. Her happiness is symbolic of what you don't have. Your life is a mess while hers is blooming. Whatever emotion you're feeling, don't judge it. Explore it with curiosity. To help you express it further, write it down.

Don't Judge Your Feelings: This one is difficult because we do it so often it's become a habit that's difficult to break. For example, you might feel angry about something, but instead of exploring the feeling of anger, you feel ashamed because you think you should be able to control your anger better. You feel sad because you can't go on vacation for your birthday, but that sadness turns to guilt because there are people starving in the world, but you're acting like a spoiled brat because you can't go jet-setting across the globe. Or you might feel abandoned because some of your friends didn't like an Instagram post that was really important to you, but you suppress the feeling because you don't want to feel like you're being childish. Do you get my point?

It's difficult, but try and be compassionate with yourself, and engage with your feelings without explaining them away, getting distracted by another emotion, or telling yourself how much of a bad person you are for feeling like this. It's important to understand that your feelings are not facts. Just because you've felt something doesn't make it true, and in most cases, they're contradictory. You give yourself permission to feel your feelings when you don't judge them.

What Are Your Feelings Telling You: Psychology professor John Grych from Marquette University states that emotions are useful because they help us identify what we need so that we can start working on what we need to do to fulfill that need. Evaluating our feelings isn't about acting on them, it's about finding ways to cope with them. Constant anxiety about your future might be a sign that you need to stop social media use for a while and get yourself together. Or you might be irritated all the time because it's time for you to move out of your parents' house.

Mindful and Safe Expression: There is nothing wrong with expressing your emotions as long as it's done in a mindful and safe way. Do you need to release your frustration through crying? Speak to a friend? Perhaps you going for a run will help you release anger? How you express your emotions is up to you. Either way, it's important to express how you feel because that's how you get relief. Expression is how you free yourself from falling into the destructive behaviors that come with suppressing your emotions.

Use Distractions: When you are not in a safe environment to express your emotions, use distractions to divert your attention elsewhere until you are in a safe place to deal with your emotions. For example, if you've had an argument with your sister while you were at work, going back into the office and bursting into tears at your desk is unprofessional. There are plenty of ways you can distract yourself from your emotions, such as reading a book, meditation, breathing exercises, or playing with a pet.

Find Ways to Relax

You've probably just come out of the worst season of your life; the trauma you've endured and the stress you are still facing manifests as psychological and physical tension. Feeling psychologically tense increases physical tension and vice versa. Conversely, relaxing helps release tension in the body so that you can relax physically; relaxing the body helps relieve psychological stress. There are several techniques you can implement to help you relax both physically and mentally.

Physical Relaxation: Physical relaxation interrupts and reverses the stress response. This blocks the negative feedback cycle that causes the mind to respond to stress by sending the body a message to respond to the stress. The response is tension in the body, and this increases emotional stress. I found the following techniques very helpful for relieving tension in the body:

- Exercise
- Progressive muscle relaxation
- Breathing exercises

Exercise: Mental health professionals often use exercise as a part of the treatment plan for their patients. Exercise alleviates many of the symptoms associated with depression, such as low energy, anger, tension, and fatigue. For people suffering from post-traumatic stress disorder, or conditions related to anxiety, exercise can be an effective way to release worry, fear, and built-up frustration. Exercise also helps protect the body against panic attacks.

In general, studies have found that exercise improves sleep quality, boosts energy levels, and enhances mood. There are several reasons why exercise helps to improve the psychological well-being of those who participate in it. They include:

- Protects against stress
- Improves mental health
- Boosts confidence

- A distraction from negative thoughts
- Decreases stress hormone levels

Types of Exercise: There are several types of exercise you can participate in; what you choose is up to you. But these are the ones I've found most helpful:

Yoga: Hatha yoga is the most common form of yoga. It involves controlled breathing, physical poses, and periods of meditation. Yoga helps heal the mind and body; I noticed the effects immediately.

Tai Chi: This ancient Chinese martial art combines rhythmic breathing, meditation, and a series of graceful and slow body movements called forms. Studies have found that Tai Chi helps to:

- Boost self-esteem
- Improve depression
- Reduce anxiety
- Lower blood pressure
- Reduce stress

Aerobic Exercise: An increasing number of studies have found that regular aerobic exercise such as swimming, cycling, or running improves psychological health.

Before You Start: Jumping on a bike or going for a run sounds simple enough, but if you're not used to exercising, or if you have a health condition, it's best that you visit your doctor to get some advice about the best form of exercise for you.

Make a Plan: Once you've got the all-clear from your doctor, the next step is to make a plan. I found exercise difficult to get into because I wasn't used to it. If I told myself I'd go in the morning before work, I'd hit the snooze button until it was too late for me to go. If I told myself I was going to go after work, I'd make the excuse I was too tired. So you need to make a plan and stick to it. To start, I had to admit to myself that I was being slightly ambitious by going to the gym, so I started out with brisk walks three times a week. I'd go first thing in the morning to get it out of the way. I would leave my sneakers by my bedroom door so they were the first thing I saw when I woke up in the morning. As soon as I opened my eyes, the sight of my sneakers acted as a trigger. I got up, got dressed, and went for a walk. I put a timer on and listened to motivational music as I walked.

Progressive Muscle Relaxation: This simple muscle relaxation technique helps reduce tension in the body and relieve psychological stress. It involves tensing and then releasing all the large muscle groups in your body. You'll need at least 15 minutes to complete the entire exercise so block out some time when you know you are not going to be disturbed. I would also advise setting an alarm so you know when to stop.

- Sit or lie in a comfortable position (I found it easier to lie down).

- Make sure your legs and arms are uncrossed so that it's easier for you to relax.

- Tense all the muscles in your face, close your eyes as tight as you can. While your face is in a tight grimace, mentally count to eight seconds at the same time as taking a deep breath.

- Release the tension, breathe out slowly, and completely relax your face. Rest for a couple of seconds before moving on to the next step.

- Tense your neck and shoulders, take a deep breath in while you count to eight.

- Breathe out and relax your neck and shoulders.

- Continue the process by working on your chest, stomach, right arm, right hand by making a fist, left arm, left hand by making a fist, buttocks, right leg, right foot, left leg, and left foot.

Breathing Exercises: When you're stressed out and frustrated, your breathing becomes shallow. This involves taking quick, short breaths, which signal to the brain that you are stressed, and the chemicals cortisol and adrenaline are released, which make you feel even more stressed. Slow, deep breathing shuts down the stress response, and your body returns to a relaxed state. Here are three breathing exercises that I've found extremely helpful:

A Long Exhale: It's common to hear people say "take a deep breath" when they're stressed or angry. But sometimes that doesn't work; in fact, if you take a lot of deep breaths in too quickly, it can cause you to hyperventilate. Therefore, the most effective way to relax is to breathe out deeply.

- Sit in a comfortable position.
- Set an alarm clock for five minutes.
- Breathe all the air out of your lungs and naturally allow your lungs to inhale.
- Take a deep breath in for four seconds.
- Breathe out for six seconds.
- Repeat this until your alarm goes off.

Belly Breathing: When you breathe from your diaphragm, you strengthen the lungs, which allows you to hold more air.

- Sit or lie in a comfortable position.
- Set your alarm clock for ten minutes.
- Place one hand just beneath your rib cage and the other hand on top of your heart.
- Breathe in and out through your nose, paying attention to how your chest and stomach move

as you breathe. You will most likely notice that your chest moves when you breathe and not your stomach.

- The aim of belly breathing is to get your stomach to move and not your chest.
- To start, place one hand just above your belly button, and put the other hand on your chest.
- As you take a deep breath in through your nose, your belly should rise, and your chest should stay still.
- Breathe out through your lips while you purse them together.
- Push all the air out at the end of the breath by engaging your stomach muscles.
- Repeat the exercise until your alarm goes off.

Equal Breathing: This breathing exercise originates from the ancient practice of pranayama yoga. It involves inhaling and exhaling for the same amount of time.

- Sit or lie in a comfortable position.
- Set your alarm clock for five minutes.
- Close your eyes and focus on your normal breathing pattern for a few seconds.
- Take a deep breath through your nose and count to four.

- Breathe out through your mouth and count to four.
- As you breathe in and out, keep your mind focused on how your lungs feel empty and full.
- Repeat the exercise until your alarm goes off.

Mental Relaxation: Mental relaxation involves freeing your mind from all those worrying and anxious thoughts. I've found that the following works best for me:

- Meditation
- Visualization
- Journaling

Meditation: Not only does meditation give you a sense of peace and calm, but it has also been scientifically proven to improve your emotional well-being by reducing negative emotions, helping you focus on the present, and increasing self-awareness. Here are a couple of meditation techniques I find helpful:

Metta Meditation: You will also hear metta meditation referred to as "loving-kindness" meditation, and that's exactly what you need in your life right about now after all the hell you've just been through. The main aim is to help you develop an attitude of love and kindness towards stressful situations and the people who have caused you pain. This type of meditation helps individuals who have been affected by:

- Interpersonal conflict
- Resentment
- Frustration
- Anger

Additionally, research suggests that this type of meditation is linked to an increase in positive emotions and reduced post-traumatic stress disorder, anxiety, and depression. Here is how to get started:

- Set your alarm clock for five minutes.
- Sit in a comfortable position, relax your muscles, close your eyes, and start taking deep breaths.
- Imagine that you're experiencing inner peace and total physical and emotional wellness. You love yourself perfectly; you are thankful for who you are because everything about you is perfect.
- Each time you breathe out, imagine breathing out tension.
- Each time you breathe in, imagine breathing in love and gratitude.
- Repeat positive phrases to yourself such as:
  o "I am a giver and receiver of appreciation today."
  o "I am strong, peaceful, and healthy."

- o "I am safe."
- o "I am happy."
- Sit in the feelings of love, self-compassion, and warmth for a few minutes.
- If your mind starts to wander, gently bring it back to feelings of love, warmth, and self-compassion.

Mindfulness Meditation: Mindfulness meditation helps you remain present and aware in the moment. Instead of dwelling on the abusive relationship you've just left or thinking about how difficult it's going to be to trust anyone again, mindfulness encourages you to focus on your now. The meditation also involves eliminating any judgment about what you are currently experiencing. You can practice mindfulness meditation at any time, no matter where you are. Several studies have found that there are many benefits to mindfulness. These include:

- Reduced emotional and impulsive reactions
- Improved memory
- Less focus on negative emotions
- Improved relationship satisfaction

Here are some tips on getting started:

- Get into a seated position (you can stand if you're not at home).

- If you are sitting on the floor, cross your legs. If you're sitting on a chair, place your feet flat on the floor.
- Keep your upper body straight but not stiff.
- Place your hands on top of your legs.
- Remain in the position for a few seconds while you focus on your breath.
- As you breathe in and out, say the words "follow it" in your mind.
- Focus on your breathing by paying attention to the way your stomach rises and falls with each breath and all the other aspects of breathing, such as sound and feeling.
- When your mind wanders, bring your attention back to your breath.
- If you need to make a physical adjustment, such as move your foot or your arm, pause and think about it before doing so.
- After being in this state for a few minutes, direct your focus to your environment, the sounds, and what you can see. Notice your thoughts and your emotions. How does your body feel?
- Take a moment to pause and think about how you're going to continue with your day.

Zen Meditation: You will also hear zen meditation referred to as "zazen." It involves getting into a comfortable position, focusing on your breathing, and mindfully observing your thoughts without judging them. Here are some tips on getting started:

- Set an alarm clock for two minutes.
- Get into a comfortable seated position with your legs crossed and your back straight. You can either close your eyes or focus them on a single point in the room.
- Relax your facial muscles and jaw. Pay attention to any tension you feel in these areas. If you feel any tension, give your face a massage with your fingers.
- Focus on your breath by breathing in and out through your nose.
- Pay attention to the temperature sensations as your breath passes through your body, the sound of your breath, and your natural rhythmic breathing.
- Your mind will wander during this time. Allow your thoughts to pass by, redirecting your focus to your breathing.
- One way to regain focus is to count your breaths.

Visualization: Visualization is a powerful technique that requires you to see what you want even if you don't have it. The energy you put into the visualization process will help shift your life into a new dimension. Most people use visualization to reach material or personal goals. I used it to overcome negative emotions and think more positive thoughts. Here are some tips on how you can visualize your way out of the pain you're feeling:

- Set your alarm clock for five minutes.
- Sit or lie in a comfortable position.
- Close your eyes and start taking slow, deep breaths to relax your body.
- Imagine you are at a place where you feel calm and content. This could be a beach, on top of a mountain, a vacation destination, etc.
- Add as much detail to your visualization by using your senses. What can you smell? What can you hear? What can you feel?
- As you enter deeper into your vision, imagine yourself feeling more peaceful and calmer.
- Keep taking slow, deep breaths as you immerse yourself in the scene you've created, experiencing it with all your senses.
- As you breathe in, imagine harmony and peace entering your body. As you breathe out, imagine distress, tension, and exhaustion leaving your body.
- Remain in this state until your alarm clock goes off.

Mood Journaling: Since I love to write, I've found journaling very helpful. However, if writing isn't your thing, you can skip it. Studies have found that it helps improve mood, boosts the immune system, and alleviates stress. I can't tell you whether it's improved my immune system, but I can definitely say it helped with my mood and stress levels. Here are some tips to get you started:

The first step is to get yourself a blank journal and write out a list with the following headings:

- Emotion name
- What caused the emotion?
- Actions or behaviors that this emotion led to
- Is this emotion justified considering the situation?
- Is this situation something I can tolerate, or do I need to solve it? If so, how?

Emotion Name

According to psychologists, there are eight primary emotions, and the underlying cause of your behavior is often attached to one of the following:

- **Anger:** Violence, resentment, hostility, irritability, wrath, outrage, fury
- **Shame:** Contrition, regret, remorse, chagrin, embarrassment, guilt
- **Disgust:** Revulsion, distaste, aversion, scorn, disdain, contempt

- **Surprise:** Wonder, astound, amazement, astonishment, shock
- **Interest:** Devotion, love, affection, kindness, trust, friendliness, acceptance
- **Joy:** Ecstasy, thrill, pride, delight, bliss, relief, happiness, enjoyment
- **Fear:** Panic, fright, dread, nervousness, apprehension, anxiety
- **Sadness:** Depression, loneliness, despair, melancholy, gloom, sorrow, grief

Additionally, here are some other emotions you might be feeling: Worthless, excited, uncomfortable, worried, trapped, tense, miserable, energetic, depressed, insecure, inadequate, hurt, satisfied, bored, relieved, proud, overwhelmed, foolish, bitter, comfortable, confused.

What caused the emotion?

When we step back and self-reflect, we can pinpoint the situation that fueled the emotion. On the surface, your emotion might not make sense until you dig a little deeper. For example, you got angry because your kids left their dishes in the sink despite the fact that you've told them multiple times to wash them. You have every right to be angry if you feel your children are disrespecting you. Additionally, you should discipline them if they are not following the rules. However, the underlying cause of your anger is because your ex-partner never listened to you. He took great pleasure in doing everything he knew would upset you. So when it appears that people are not listening to you, you subconsciously think they are doing it on purpose to upset you in the same way as your ex-partner.

Actions or behaviors that this emotion lead to

It's human nature to react to your emotions. At times, this will lead to beautiful expressions of joy, gratitude, or love. But other times, it means having a crying fest in the bathroom or screaming at the driver who cut you off on the road. What did your action or behavior look like today?

Is this emotion justified considering the situation?

Therapists refer to this step as "checking the facts." Are your emotional responses justified considering the situation? You should also think about the scale of your response. It might help to look at the situation objectively and think about the advice you'd give to a friend if they were in a similar situation.

Is this situation something I can tolerate, or do I need to solve it? If so, how?

If your emotion was a negative one, you will need to think about what you're going to do about it. There are some situations you'll be able to change, and others you won't. Whatever you have control over, make an action plan. If a friend said something to upset you, arrange to have a conversation with them so you can talk about how you feel. If you've noticed some health symptoms, call your doctor and book an appointment. However, there are some circumstances that are out of your control. In this instance, experts advise that you implement the concept of "distress tolerance." This relates to our capacity to deal with difficult emotions. Think about the healthy coping mechanisms you have available—for example, exercise, meditation, or deep breathing—and then become diligent in implementing them. If you react to your triggers as soon as you're exposed to them and your actions don't align with the trigger (for example, the train was late so it sent you into a rage), and that messed up your whole day, you should practice your coping mechanism at that moment to keep yourself calm. In your mood journal, write out a game plan to help when negative emotions arise.

Okay, so you've processed the trauma...now what? It's time to start your recovery journey.

Chapter 6: Starting Your Recovery Journey

"The greater the obstacle, the more glory in overcoming it." ~ Moliere

Before I begin, give yourself a round of applause for making it this far! Trust and do believe there are a lot of people who either stay in an abusive relationship because they can't imagine living any other way, or they build skyscraper-sized walls around themselves, refuse to heal, and refuse to let anyone help them. They end up bitter and miserable, and even though they are no longer in an abusive relationship, they never recover from the trauma. But I know that recovery is possible because I've recovered. I'm happy, healthy, and in a beautiful relationship with a man who doesn't have a narcissistic bone in his body. The journey is going to be a difficult one, but I'm walking with you and cheering you on, so let's go...

Go Through the Grieving Process

One of the most devastating aspects of narcissistic abuse is that you can't forget the good days. During my recovery process, there were days when I wished I could have had a lobotomy to wipe out all the memories because they kept me chained to him in a very unhealthy way. When I got lonely, I remembered the vacations he took me on, the gifts he bought me, how safe and secure I felt when he wrapped me in his arms. It was those good times that I longed for when we were together, and it was those good times I longed for when we broke up. When someone has been a part of your life for so long and they leave, the feeling is the same as when a loved one dies, and it's important that you go through the entire grieving process.

A breakup can be one of the most emotional and stressful experiences in life. Your whole world is turned upside down, and this triggers unsettling and painful emotions. Despite the abuse, it represents a loss of what could have been. You and your partner shared commitments and dreams. You had high hopes for the future. Now, you've been launched into unchartered territory. Everything is disrupted—your relationships with extended family and mutual friends, your home, your responsibilities, your routine. Now you don't know what the future will look like. Will you end up alone? Will you ever be able to trust anyone else? What will your life be like now? I found that the feeling of this uncertainty was worse than being in an abusive relationship, and you might too.

Recovering from a breakup and the scars of emotional abuse is going to take time; however, it's important to keep reminding yourself that you will recover, this difficult experience won't be the end of you, it doesn't define you, and there are better days ahead. To begin, according to psychiatrist Elisabeth Kubler Ross, there are five stages of grief you will go through:

Denial: The first stage in the grief process is denial. You are in so much pain because of the breakup that denying it happened is the only way to cope. At the same time as trying to come to terms with the emotional pain of the breakup, you are also trying to process the reality of your loss. Despite the abuse, your partner was an important part of your life, and it's hard to believe he's no longer there. In the moment of loss, there is a complete shift in your reality, and you'll find yourself contemplating how you can keep going without this person in your life. There's a lot to take in and a lot of painful emotions to walk through. Denial takes us through this process one step at a time so you don't feel overwhelmed by your emotions. Not only is denial a way of pretending that the breakup hasn't happened, but it's also how we try and understand and absorb what's happening.

Anger: Anger is a common emotion experienced when grieving. At the same time as going through extreme emotional discomfort, you are also trying to get used to a new reality. There is so much to take in that anger feels like the only emotional outlet available to you. You will feel anger as soon as you start processing emotions related to loss. I found the anger stage extremely difficult because my friends and family kept their distance during this time. I felt isolated and alone, but it was only once I'd got to the other side and could think rationally that I realized my friends and family weren't being dismissive. The reality is that no one wants to be around angry people.

Bargaining: One of the coping mechanisms for dealing with loss is bargaining. You will so desperately want to free yourself from the pain of losing your partner that you'll start thinking about bargaining tools. They typically come in the form of promises such as:

- God, if you can change [name of your ex-partner], I promise I'll never be angry again.
- I promise to become a better person if I can get back together with [name of ex-partner].
- I'll live a life of total gratitude if I can just get back together with [name of ex-partner].

The bargaining process is often directed at a higher power or some other spiritual entity because it's at this moment that we become acutely aware of our humanity. You feel completely powerless to change your situation, but something bigger than you might be able to intervene. The bargaining process will give you a false sense of control over something that feels so out of your control. The bargaining process also involves focusing on your regrets or personal faults. You might think about times when you had arguments or disagreements with your partner, and you feel that if you'd just done as she'd asked, the relationship would not have come to an end. You will want to turn back the hands of time and redo those moments.

Depression: As you process your grief, you'll get to a point when you stop imagining what could have been, and you'll start to confront the reality of your situation. You don't feel the need to bargain anymore because you are coming to terms with what's happened to you. During this time, you'll start feeling the loss of your partner more strongly because you're not panicking as much, the emotional fog that was clouding your judgment has started to clear up, and the breakup feels more unavoidable and present. In these moments, you'll start looking inwards as the sadness intensifies. You might find yourself being less sociable and isolating yourself. You won't want to talk about how you feel. You will just want to be alone with your feelings because as far as you're concerned, there's nothing anyone can do to take them away.

Acceptance: I can't tell you how long it will take before you get to a place of acceptance about your breakup. But what I can tell you is that it's the greatest feeling in the world. I woke up one morning, and I no longer felt the crushing weight of loss. I was able to get out of bed without feeling disorientated, depressed, and anxious about the future. I opened my eyes and said to myself, "Everything is going to be okay." I wasn't faking it until I made it; I actually felt as if everything was going to be okay. Acceptance means that you've stopped resisting the reality of your situation. Your partner is no longer in your life, but you are no longer struggling. It doesn't mean you've stopped feeling the pain of the loss. You will still have regrets and sadness, but the emotional survival tactics of anger, bargaining, and denial are no longer dominating forces in your life.

The Redefining Process

The wounds of narcissistic abuse can feel so deep that you don't believe you'll ever recover from them. The reality is that you can't turn back the hands of time and undo the suffering you've endured, but you can heal from the experience and use the pain as a platform to propel you into something greater. You can reclaim your identity; it will take some work on your part, but you can do it. As you go through the healing process and start working on yourself, you'll slowly start to recognize yourself in the mirror. Your smile will return, you'll regain your peace of mind. You will feel happy, and when you're ready, you may even start dating again. One of the last things Steve told me before we broke up for good was that no man will ever want me because I'm too ugly and that he was only dating me because he felt sorry for me and wanted to boost my self-esteem. He told me he was never attracted to me, hated sleeping with me, and had to think about the women he really wanted to be with to get excited. Those evil words played over and over in my head for a long time. I have spoken to many narcissistic abuse survivors whose partners said similar things to them at the end of their relationship. But regardless of what your narcissistic partner said, you deserve the best in life, and you should jolly well go out and get it because no one is going to give it to you.

Your Recovery is Your Responsibility

I spent months feeling sorry for myself after I broke up with Steve. I sat at home depressed, eating my emotions away, and blaming everyone for what I was going through. I spent hours on the phone talking about the hell I'd been through and how I didn't know how I was ever going to recover from this. I had a good support network. My friends and family wanted me to get better, but I'd become an energy vampire. There is only so much listening to your bitter woes that one person can endure before you start sounding like a broken record and getting on people's nerves. After a while, I noticed that my friends stopped answering the phone, not because they were being mean, but because they were tired of hearing the same thing over and over again. I wasn't telling them anything new other than how depressed I was because of everything that Steve had put me through. One day, my dad gave me a stern reality check. He came into my room, looked me in the eye, and said, "I know you've had a hard time, and I know you're hurting, but eventually, you will need to pull yourself out of this, or it'll kill you. Did you know that there are people who die of a broken heart? Steve took twelve years of your life. He's probably long forgotten about you. Don't let him take the rest of your life. The best years are ahead of you." The next morning, I got up, tidied my room, and went for a jog. That was the start of my recovery process.

To put it bluntly, no one is going to pull you up out of the mess you're in. The only person who has the power to heal you is you. You can read all the narcissistic abuse recovery books ever written, but if you don't do the work required for your healing, you won't heal. Think about it like this. If you had a car accident that rendered you unable to walk for some time, after the plaster cast comes off, your doctor is going to refer you to a physiotherapist. The only way you are going to regain your strength and start walking again is if you go to the physiotherapist's office and do the recommended exercises. Your legs are not going to heal on their own. Likewise, your mind isn't going to heal on its own. I spoke about trauma in Chapter 5. You've experienced a major disruption to your emotional well-being, and it's going to take some major work on your part to heal.

Healing Starts with Acknowledgment

In Alcohol Anonymous meetings, they say that the first step to curing your addiction is admitting you have it. The same applies to emotional abuse healing. You've got to acknowledge the abuse. I am assuming you've already arrived at this point, or you wouldn't be reading this book. But there are a lot of narcissistic abuse survivors who are in denial about the abuse, especially the ones who have been discarded and the narcissist walked out of their life. Women have made all types of excuses for their narcissistic partners. They will say things like, "He had a hard life. Deep down, he's really a nice person." Or "Things were really good between us before he lost his job. Everything went downhill from then. If we could get back to the way things were, we'd have the perfect relationship." One of the main reasons why women deny abuse is because of shame. Admitting that you allowed someone to treat you like that is difficult. In your mind, it means you don't believe you're worthy of true love.

It's important to remember that what happened to you isn't your fault. No one deserves abuse. But what helped me get past this hurdle was understanding that narcissistic abuse is a special type of abuse. You were literally tricked into the relationship. Think about it like this. If your ex-partner took you on a first date and started verbally abusing you the moment he picked you up, you would have told him to stop the car, got out, and blocked his number. Narcissists know how to deceive their victims, and they do it so well that you don't know it's happening until it's too late.

By labeling what happened to you as abuse, you're freeing yourself from blame. You didn't ask to get hurt. When you find the courage to say that you were abused by your narcissistic boyfriend, you are saying that he made a conscious decision to inflict unwanted harm on you. You are subconsciously passing the blame you've internalized to the narcissist so that you can start working on your healing. You should also remember that you are the only person you can control during this process. Some of your friends and family who don't understand what you're going through are going to unintentionally say some terrible things to you. During my recovery, I remember sitting at the dinner table, and my sister said, "How did you end up with someone like that and stay? I could never let anyone treat me like that. I would have left as soon as I spotted the first red flag. Please help me understand." I was so angry, I just got up and left the table, and she couldn't understand why what she said was so upsetting to me.

Let me start by saying that it's not your responsibility to explain to everyone what it means to be a victim of narcissistic abuse. If your friends and family members are so interested, they can look it up for themselves. Second of all, it's also important to remember that it was your good personality traits that made you attractive to your narcissistic boyfriend. Your empathy, your ability to love unconditionally, and your desire to see the good in everyone. Don't ever allow the abuse to take that away from you. As you keep reminding yourself that you did nothing to deserve this, treat yourself with forgiveness and compassion.

Treat Yourself with Forgiveness and Compassion

Once you've acknowledged the abuse, the next step is to forgive yourself. Now that you've established that you should be celebrated and not punished for your strengths and character traits, forgive yourself for placing the burden of abuse on your shoulders. Forgive yourself for not seeing the red flags or for seeing the red flags and ignoring them in hopes that you'd got it wrong. Forgive yourself for not packing your bags earlier. Forgive yourself for feeling that it was your fault that your love, compassion, and kindness were taken advantage of. In the same way, it's not going to be easy to forgive your ex-partner, it won't be easy to forgive yourself. Essentially, you are now looking at the relationship objectively. You are standing on the outside looking in, thinking, *How did I get myself into this situation?* But thinking about that question and the possible answers surrounding it is a waste of time and energy because you can't change the past. Recovery is about moving forward. The past acts as a rearview mirror and gives you a blueprint, so you don't make the same mistakes in the future. Your energy should be focused on putting one hundred percent effort into healing yourself. You were not in a good place for a while, but you survived. You have the strength to acknowledge the fact that you're ready to get help, and that deserves to be celebrated as you embark on your healing journey.

Remind yourself to be just as compassionate with yourself as you would with your best friend if they were in the same situation. If your friend was telling you their story, how would you react? How would you find ways to support her? How would you go out of your way to ensure your friend was made to feel comfortable? What would you say to her? Think of these things and treat yourself the same way. Refrain from condemning yourself and keep reminding yourself that you deserve compassion.

Positive Self-Talk

For months after I broke up with Steve, my nights were spent repeating all the evil words that he had spoken over my life. I told myself I was fat, ugly, stupid, incapable of finding anyone to love me. Every single insult I could think of, I repeated it to myself, and I truly believed what I was saying. As far as I was concerned, it wasn't the abuse that had made me think this way, there was something fundamentally wrong with me, and that's why I was abused. I was stupid, fat, and ugly before I met Steve. He didn't make me feel so low that I started thinking these things about myself. His voice became my internal voice.

It was only once I started therapy that I realized I had the power to turn that voice off. But I also learned that once upon a time, negative self-talk was a survival strategy for our ancestors. Negative thinking allowed cavemen to think about the worst-case scenarios so they could prepare themselves to protect their families from wild beasts. Even though we no longer need to protect ourselves from wild beasts, it is still a trait in the human psyche. We also do it to prepare for the worst-case scenario, but the problem is that it often ends up becoming our reality. The good news is that you can overcome it, but the first step is to recognize what it is and why it happens. In general, negative self-talk falls into four main categories:

Polarizing: There is no middle ground with polarizing thoughts. It's an either-or mentality. Things are only black or white, or good or bad.

Magnifying: Negative thoughts of this nature will find a problem for every solution. Anything positive is completely ignored.

Personalizing: Personalizing is when someone blames themselves for every bad thing that happens in their life, even if the situation was out of their control.

Catastrophizing: These thoughts lead a person to expect the worst no matter what the situation looks like. Even if there's a glimmer of hope, they'll dismiss it and go as far as to defy logic to rationalize why they're thinking this way.

Now that you have a better understanding of the negative thoughts that can take over your mind, you can turn them into positive thoughts. In cognitive-behavioral therapy, this process is referred to as thought replacement. As simple as it sounds, it's actually quite difficult because we are not conscious of our thoughts the majority of the time. The record of negative self-talk playing in your head comes from the subconscious mind, which makes them difficult to catch. However, every so often, you'll realize you're not speaking kindly to yourself, and it's at this point that you can make the conscious decision to change those thoughts. It was at night that I became aware of my negative inner voice; it screamed at me for hours, and I didn't know what to do to turn it off. But as soon as I learned that I could reprogram my thoughts by speaking kindly to myself, my nighttime hours became less and less traumatic. Additionally, I found repeating affirmations first thing in the morning, throughout the day, and at night really helpful. Affirmations are positive statements that you repeat to yourself. Here are some examples:

- I am a winner
- I am intelligent and beautiful
- I will meet the man of my dreams
- I deserve unconditional love
- I am beautiful, caring, and powerful
- I deserve to live my best life
- I will achieve all the goals I've set for myself

Changing your negative inner voice isn't going to happen overnight. It will take consistency and determination before you start seeing results. You are essentially replacing a bad habit with a good one, and as you continue on this journey of healing, you will develop a positive outlook that will help build your self-esteem and self-worth. Here are some tips to help you with this:

Identify Your Triggers: What situations trigger negative self-talk? Is your boss a micromanager who's very critical? Does driving past a certain park, listening to certain songs, or watching a certain TV program remind you of your partner? Identify all the triggering situations so that you can mentally prepare yourself with positive self-talk.

Monitor Your Feelings: There were some days when I felt terrible for no reason. There were no triggers, no one had upset me, and I wasn't thinking about Steve, but I just felt awful and didn't understand why. But my therapist alerted me to the fact that the subconscious mind can control your emotions without you realizing it. I had spent ten years in an abusive relationship, and everything I had experienced was playing in the background of my mind. I was advised to monitor my feelings, and if I was feeling down, think about why. Once I had recognized and labeled my feelings, the next step was to engage in positive self-talk because if you can change your thoughts, you can change how you feel.

Your Social Circle: It's easy to be a negative Nancy, to sit and complain about your situation all day without making any effort to change it. When I first broke up with Steve, I started hanging around with some old friends. They'd all experienced the perils of a bad relationship, and it made them really bitter. We would meet up for drinks and talk about how much we hated men—they were all dogs, they were all the same, and we had no hope of ever getting into a relationship again. If anyone we knew appeared to be in a loving relationship, or they were about to get married, we would sit and talk about every reason why we didn't think it would work out. At the time, I thought it made me feel better doing this. My wake-up call came when some of my more positive friends started distancing themselves from me. After months of hearing me constantly moan about what

I'd been through and what I was going through now, they got fed up with me. I didn't understand it at the time and accused them of thinking they were better than me, but once I started the healing process, I realized how important it was to keep the right company.

I would meet up with my negative Nancy friends after a therapy session and try telling them about it, but they had a problem for every solution. I wanted to give them the same hope I now had, but they weren't interested. My participation in their conversations lessened, and after a while, I stopped meeting up with them altogether. I later heard through the grapevine that I was their new topic of conversation. Apparently, I thought I was too good for them now I'd started on this "healing journey." I wasn't upset about it; in fact, I was prepared for it. My therapist warned me that it would happen. Without getting too scientific here, when you start operating on a higher frequency, your energy changes, and people are either attracted to it, or they're repelled by it. My friends were repelled by it not because they're bad people but because they weren't ready to change. I didn't hold a grudge against them for it; I understood. But ultimately, you want to surround yourself with people who are going to support your healing journey and push you to become better.

Use Humor: There's absolutely nothing funny about negative self-talk, but laughter is medicine for the soul.

Sometimes, no matter how hard you try, it's impossible to push the negative self-chatter out of your mind because your emotions are too strong in that moment. But what I found really helpful was to watch something funny, I would play a clip from my favorite comedian or watch a comedy show. It worked every time, and as soon as I started laughing, I immediately felt better. Once I started feeling better, I would say my affirmations.

You now know how to control your thoughts, and you've taken the power away from your narcissist ex-partner. You've silenced that voice and replaced it with one that empowers and uplifts you.

Take Pride in Your Survival

The goal of your narcissistic partner was to completely destroy you, but he failed. He didn't break you, he cracked you, and a crack can be fixed and transformed into something beautiful and inspiring. Despite the fact that you feel weak, it takes a very strong person to endure such high-level emotional trauma and not just survive but thrive. You are resilient and powerful, and these traits deserve to be appreciated and celebrated. You are taking the steps required to free yourself from the vicious consequences of abuse, and you are using this experience to create a better future for yourself. Focus on the change you want to make, where you want to go in life, and start taking steps in that direction.

Now it's time to put the final nail in the coffin! I wish I could put the last chapter in a bottle and give it to you to wear every time you stepped out of the house. That would be great! Unfortunately, it's not possible. But over time, if you apply the strategies in Chapter 8, you'll become a powerful narcissist repellent, and they'll run in the other direction when they see you coming!

Chapter 8: Never Again – How to Become a Narcissist Repellent

"Don't open the door to the devil, surround yourself with positive people."

~ *Cuba Gooding, Jr.*

Repeat after me: "Never again will I become a victim of narcissistic abuse!" I have been in several relationships with narcissists throughout my life. But that was because I was completely ignorant as to why I kept on attracting narcissists. For one, I didn't really know what a narcissist was. I had heard people mentioning the word. I probably said it myself a few times, only because I was repeating what I had heard. But everything changed for me once I learned everything I've written in this book. I made up my mind that I would never end up with a narcissist ever again! Not only did I have therapy, but I also thoroughly educated myself on narcissism and took the steps required to ensure I became their worst enemy and not a juicy-looking victim! This is what I came up with.

The Types of People Narcissists Are Attracted To

Narcissists are very selective in who they date. They look for a special kind of person, and you don't want to be that person again. So before I tell you how to become a narcissist repellent, you need to know what a narcissist is looking for in their victim.

Successful but Insecure: I don't believe there is a person on the planet who is fully confident in who they are. It always shocks you when you hear your favorite celebrity with the perfect body talk about their insecurities. There's nothing wrong with being a bit insecure as long as it's not the driving force behind your life. Insecurities should keep you on your toes so that you're constantly striving to become the best version of yourself. Successful, attractive, and well-put-together people with slight insecurities are the narcissist's delight. They fit the perfect template for what the narcissist will think makes them look good. Narcissistic men are attracted to beautiful and accomplished women, not because it's natural to admire these traits, and they genuinely have an interest in such women, but because her accomplishments and appearance fuel his ego.

However, the narcissist also wants a woman who isn't too confident because he wants to be the boss of the relationship. So, if he gets a whiff that you're insecure, he'll be that much more attracted to you because you won't threaten his success even if it's in his head. While it feels slightly uncomfortable to admit your insecurities, owning them and taking the necessary steps to boost your self-confidence will help you become a narcissist repellent.

You Don't Like Conflict: In general, people don't like conflict. We'd all rather live in a happy, peaceful world than spend our time bickering all day. However, sometimes conflict is necessary because you can't just allow people to walk all over you. Of course, you should pick your battles wisely and refrain from reacting to every offense. However, according to body language expert Patti Wood, narcissists are drawn to people who won't cause them much harm but will cooperate with them on every level. If you tend to submit to the demands and wishes of people in your personal life or your coworkers for the sake of avoiding conflict, you will definitely fit the ideal profile for what a narcissist is looking for in a partner. It's important to compromise in a relationship, but being a doormat is setting yourself up to be devoured by a narcissist.

You're a People Pleaser: Of course, we want to make the person we are dating happy, but it becomes unhealthy if meeting someone else's needs is done at the expense of your own well-being. A narcissist wants a partner who is going to give them constant emotional validation and attention no matter what it costs them. Author and psychotherapist Karen Koenig says that narcissists are attracted to people who don't have a strong sense of self, and because of this, they feel more comfortable taking care of someone else's needs than their own.

You Are Empathetic: Narcissists are attracted to empathetic people for several reasons. First, they are a good source of supply because they have a deep desire to help others. This sets off a chain reaction. They'll unknowingly feed the narcissist's ego by complimenting them all the time, thinking that they are being a source of encouragement. When the narcissists launch their devaluing attack, they'll stick around longer than the average person because people with high empathy are less likely to see what's happening to them as abuse, but they'll put it down to the narcissist having a bad day. Additionally, narcissists lack empathy, so they enjoy being around people who can give them what they don't have.

How to Become a Narcissist Repellent

For most of you reading this, everything I've just mentioned is nothing new to you. You can probably recognize yourself in at least one of the traits narcissists are attracted to. Let me start by saying this isn't about changing who you fundamentally are as a person. It's about protecting yourself so that you are never again exposed to the horrors of narcissistic abuse. I can tell you with confidence that it works because I went from being a narcissist magnet to a narcissist repellent. I kept on jumping in and out of relationships with narcissists, and it wasn't until I made these changes in my life that I met a normal guy.

Become the Best Version of Yourself

When you are confident in who you are and what you stand for, no one can take that away from you. Becoming the best version of yourself eliminates the need to have people in your life who don't value you. If you love yourself, why on Earth are you going to tolerate someone who doesn't love you the way you deserve to be loved? Here are some tips on how to become the best version of yourself.

Write the Vision: To start, you need to know what the best version of yourself looks like. Get a notepad and pen and write out your ideal life. Don't compromise and don't leave things out because, deep down, you think your dreams are too big for you. There's no such thing as impossible. Whatever life you want, you can attain it if you're willing to put in the work. Once you've refined what your ideal self looks like, write out a plan of how you intend to get there. Do you need to gain some qualifications, lose weight, start your own business? Whatever it is, write it down and start working towards it. But the key is to become so relentless about it that you refuse to let anything or anyone stop you from achieving your goals. Crystalizing your vision about who you want to be is the first step to becoming a narcissist repellent because when you become an unstoppable force of nature, you are not going to want people in your life who are going to derail you.

Look Good: Michelle Obama said it best: "When you look good, you feel good." There's absolutely nothing wrong with throwing your hair in a bun, wearing a onesie, and Netflix and chilling. But you should do your best to make an effort with your physical appearance. Everyone knows there's a connection between looking good and feeling good because we've all experienced it. You've got more pep in your step when you turn up to your presentation rocking a blowout or a three-piece suit. Or you feel more excited and flirtier when you hit the town in your favorite dress with your favorite shade of lipstick to match. On the flip side, you know how you felt when you had to rush your beauty routine because you slept through your alarm. Or how about highlights or a haircut that turned out disastrous? All these feelings are normal and valid, but there is actually a growing body of research that suggests there are psychological benefits to looking good.

Self-care routines that focus on beauty, sleep habits, skincare, and exercise make people feel healthier, happier, and more in control of their daily lives. Such habits do more than elevate a person's physical appearance. Self-care is how you keep your inner and outer self happy, thriving, and healthy. It's really important that we spend time on self-care rituals, such as applying your favorite face mask or getting the occasional spa treatment. We all have habitual behavioral patterns in life that will determine how we feel. How about making looking good one of them? Here are some tips on how you can do this:

- **Conform to Your Own Beauty Standards:** We live in a very controlling world that directly or indirectly teaches us how to think, act, and look. But these ideals are constantly changing. A few years ago, it was considered hideous to have a big butt, full lips, and a curvaceous figure; today, because of celebrities such as Beyoncé, Kim Kardashian, and Jennifer Lopez, women are now paying thousands of dollars for these features. Prior to that, the trend was to be stick-thin and skeletal-looking. Catwalks around the world called it "heroin chic." If society sets the beauty standards and you try and conform to them, you're going to spend your life in a perpetual state of dissatisfaction. The remedy for this is to conform to your own standards of beauty. Granted, there's no such thing as perfection. We all have our insecurities, but the key is not to allow those insecurities to define you.

- **Wear Flattering Clothes:** Flattering clothes are always going to make you feel more comfortable, especially when you haven't reached your weight loss goals. I remember the days when I had started putting on weight, I was in complete denial that my clothes were now two sizes too small, and I would squeeze myself into skirts and jeans that I had no business wearing! I knew the clothes were too tight, and I felt terribly uncomfortable when I went out, choosing to keep my coat on so I wouldn't reveal the fact that I couldn't breathe in my skinny jeans! When I started my weight loss journey, I didn't throw out my old clothes; I kept them as a source of inspiration because I was determined to fit into them. But in the meantime, I went out and bought clothes that were flattering to my current size, and even though I knew I was overweight, I felt a lot more confident wearing clothes that actually fit me. Additionally, don't feel pressured into conforming to the latest fashion craze. I have a very distinct and unique style. I developed it years ago, and it suits me. I get plenty of compliments when I go out, and that's what works for me. So do you, boo! Flex in your own style and refuse to allow anyone to dictate how you dress.

- **Exercise:** Even if you don't need to lose weight, exercise is a great way to look good. You will hear it referred to as the fountain of youth because of the powerful impact it has on our mental and physical well-being. Exercise increases blood flow, which provides the body with more oxygen, helping to keep the skin cells healthy. Do you have a terrible habit of slouching? Incorporating some strength training into your exercise routine will help strengthen the muscles in that area and improve your posture.

- **Have a Photoshoot:** There is nothing better than a professional photo shoot to make you feel better about yourself. You can capture your ideal of perfection in a series of photos that make you look spectacular. Additionally, when you add those pictures to your professional profiles, you'll attract the high-quality job or clients you know you deserve.

Stop Being so Quick to Praise People

As you know, narcissists expect and need praise from people. When we were out, and Steve met anyone new, he spent the entire time talking about his accomplishments, the accolades he had received, and everything he thought made himself an Adonis in his imaginary world. When I look back, it was actually quite embarrassing. Although he did get a lot of listening ears, I could tell by some of their expressions that they weren't impressed. It's normal to congratulate someone on their achievements; however, when you start dating again, and you start off admiring your love interest by giving them praise, if they're a narcissist, it will signal to them that you are a potential source of supply. Because of my sensitive nature, I meet narcissists all the time. We'll go on a date, and I'll spot their narcissistic tendencies as soon as they start talking about their achievements. Here are some tips on how to get around this:

- If you meet someone who keeps going on about their accomplishments, acknowledge what they've said, and then change the subject. For example, you could say something like, "That's fantastic! Good for you! I got some pretty amazing stuff done too. Oh my goodness, did you see what happened in Florida last night?"

- If your date keeps bringing the conversation back to their achievements, wait until there's a break in the conversation, take a look at your watch, and say you've got to excuse yourself.

I've lost count of the number of times I've done this, and it works like a charm. The face on a narcissist when they realize they're not going to get what they want out of you is priceless. And walking away from a date with them is epic!

Become an Expert in Constructive Criticism

Narcissists don't like to hear any form of criticism because it disrupts their alternate reality of believing they're perfect human beings. Criticizing a narcissist is like exposing a vampire to light; they run and hide. For example:

- If the narcissist takes you out on a bowling date and he misses a shot, you could say something like, "Even though you've got a strong arm, you're not flicking your wrist in the right way, which is why you keep missing."

- There is no need to be mean or nasty. Avoid saying things like, "That shirt exposes your fat rolls." Or "Your car doesn't match your grandiose personality; I think you might want to consider getting a new one." Remember, it's not about stooping down to the narcissist's level. You're better than that. Say something helpful even if the narcissist doesn't accept the help.

Become More Confident

True confidence comes from within. It means that you are happy and content with life, you are not defined by your circumstances, and you understand that life is about making the most out of the cards you've been dealt. Narcissists don't have this ability, and they deeply resent people who do. Despite the bitter smiles they may crack every so often, narcissists are vengeful people who want to completely crush and destroy the souls of their victims. However, confident people are difficult to break, and one thing narcissists don't like doing is working. They want an easy ride, and so as soon as they smell confidence, they're off! Here are some tips on how you can become more confident.

Name It and Shame It! In order to subdue the demon, you've got to name it. What areas of your life do you lack confidence in? When do you doubt yourself and feel negative emotions taking over? What abilities and skills are limiting you, and what would you like to have more confidence in? Once you know what you're dealing with, it won't feel so overwhelming because you'll know what you're working with. So, before you start on your journey to boost your confidence, write down everything you want to have more confidence in.

What Makes You Feel Confident? Think about the times in your life when you've felt the most confident. Was it when you were playing on the school netball team? Singing in the choir? Giving a speech? Now think about why you felt so empowered during those times. Was it the feeling? The environment? Something you did? Or the compliments you received? The clearer you are on this, the easier it will be for you to tap into it when you need it the most.

Be Your Authentic Self: One of the easiest ways to lose confidence is to try and be someone you're not. You are who you are for a reason, and that's because there's no one else on the planet who can do what you do. When you are trying to be a counterfeit of someone else, everything in you will resist it, and you'll feel terribly uncomfortable. The more you get to know yourself and understand your values, the easier it will be to gain confidence. When you are trying to be someone you're not, you are literally running away from yourself and trying to step into someone else's shoes. Confidence will evade you if it can't communicate with your authentic self.

One Hundred Percent Smart: When my son was in 5th grade, his teacher gave him homework called 100% smart. The students were asked to make a pie chart and identify how smart they thought they were in these areas: Art, music, word, math, body, self, people. For example, my son said he was 35% math smart but only 10% word smart. This gave my son a lot of insight into his strengths and weaknesses, and it's something I've shared with friends ever since. He realized that even though he didn't have much confidence in putting words together, he excelled in a lot of other areas. You are no different. You might not feel confident speaking in front of audiences, but you've got a fantastic writing ability, or you're a great cook. Most of us spend way too much time focusing on what we're not good at instead of acknowledging our skills and talents and focusing on developing them.

Get Out of the Comparison Trap: Nothing robs you of your confidence more than comparing yourself to people. Whether it's friends, family, or celebrities, social media has given us access to people's lives like never before. However, what we fail to realize is that we are only seeing what they want to show us, and that's the best version of themselves. In general, people aren't posting about how they spent hours in bed crying because they feel alone and depressed. Nevertheless, regardless of what's being posted on social media, the only person you should be comparing yourself with is the person you were yesterday and the person you are today. Your goal should be to become the best version of yourself. Stop focusing on the fact that your friends just bought a new house, a new car, or got a promotion. Everyone's journey is different. If you feel envious because you don't have these things, it's a sign you need to work harder to achieve what you want.

Develop Your Skills: Growth doesn't happen in your comfort zone. If you want to become better, you've got to be willing to do something extra. One of the things I did when I started my healing journey was take a creative writing course. I always knew I had a writing gift because that's what I loved to do. But just because you've got a gift doesn't mean you can't improve it. Think about it like this. All athletes are naturally gifted, but they spend the majority of their time training to perfect their skills. Take the same approach to whatever you're naturally good at.

Practice Gratitude: It's easy to look at what we don't have and feel frustrated and depressed. That frustration and depression are intensified when you turn on the TV, radio, or open a newspaper and get exposed to all the chaos that's happening in the world. When we focus on everything that's wrong in our lives, we forget about or minimize the things that are right in our lives. When I started practicing gratitude, my spirit came alive, and my mind started zoning in on all the wonderful things I have in my life and in the world. It's a simple exercise that you can do as soon as you wake up in the morning and just before you go to bed at night. Get a journal and a pen and write down three things you're grateful for. Feel the emotion of gratitude and remain in that feeling for five minutes.

And that's all, folks! If you've applied all the strategies I've mentioned in this chapter, you are now officially a narcissist repellent!

Conclusion

"I can't change the direction of the wind. But I can adjust my sails to always reach my destination." ~ *Jimmy Dean*

My father was probably the most intelligent man I have ever known. He knew something about everything. Most children grow up with pets; I was raised with books! We had an entire library in our house. On my birthday, guess what I got as a gift? A book! My dad's favorite topic was self-development. He had all the advice in the world about becoming the best version of yourself and reaching your full potential. But it wasn't until I got to my late teenage years that I realized that he didn't apply any of the information he learned. He was always talking about his dreams, but I only knew them as conversations. I never saw them come to life. His death was a sad one because I knew that he took his dreams to the grave with him.

In my later years, I learned that wisdom isn't about having a lot of knowledge but the application of it. And that's what I want to leave with you. I don't refer to myself as a narcissistic abuse survivor—I'm a narcissistic abuse thriver! I rose out of the ashes of despair and used the pain I'd experienced to propel myself into my purpose. People look at me today and admire my success, and many try and tap into my potential, thinking that if they hang around me long enough, I'll just rub off on them. But it doesn't work like that. What am I trying to tell you? That reading this book isn't going to get you unstuck if you don't apply what you've read. Recovery from narcissistic abuse is a long and painful process, but you've got to put in the work.

I don't know how long any of you reading this have been in a relationship with a narcissist, but I do know that time is not a factor when it comes to emotional damage. According to experts, the worst of it can happen on the first day of the abuse. All it takes is one word to destroy a person's soul and change the entire trajectory of their life. Words are powerful, and they stick. The damage is deep-rooted, and you'll need to work extremely hard to uproot it. Yes, you are going to have support from friends and family members who want to see you heal from your brokenness, but ultimately, the healing process is your responsibility. It sounds harsh, but that's the reality of the situation.

I'd also like to stress that you should remain single until you're fully recovered. One of the biggest mistakes I ever made was to start dating again halfway through my healing journey. And guess what happened? I ended up with another narcissist! I was lonely, desperate for some company, in therapy, and had seen some improvements emotionally...but I was far from healed. Even though I got out of the relationship as soon as I realized he was a narcissist, I had to start my healing process from scratch. Physically, you can compare it to starting a diet, losing most of the weight, relapsing, and putting it back on again. You'll know what you need to do to lose the weight again, but you'll be kicking yourself for allowing it to get this far in the first place. So please stay single until you are ready. And you'll know when that time has arrived; you'll feel it in your gut.

Now it's time to soar... I wish you every success as you begin your recovery journey from narcissistic abuse!

Thank you

Before you go, I just wanted to say thank you for purchasing my book. I poured a ton of time into this book and shared a lot of my personal experiences and those of people I spoke to when compiling the book to show you that you're not alone in this, and a beautiful and fulfilling life where you can feel safe and free from abuse is within your grasp.

You just need to reach out and make it happen. Every journey, even one along the road to recovery, starts with a single step. This is your permission to take yours.

It's also a fantastic thought to me that you could have picked from dozens of other books on the same topic, but you took a chance and chose this one.

So, a HUGE thanks to you for getting this book and for reading all the way to the end.

Now I wanted to ask you for a small favor. Could you please consider posting a review on the platform? Your reviews are one of the easiest ways to support the work of independent authors, and it's incredible to go online and see all the amazing support this work has received. I love hearing from you, and hearing your feedback inspires me to write more in the future and helps me to identify what to do better and how to be the best writer I can.

This feedback will help me continue to write the type of books that will help you get the results you want. So if you enjoyed it, please let me know.

Also by Amy White

- Digital Minimalism in Everyday Life: Overcome Technology Addiction, Declutter Your Mind, and Reclaim Your Freedom

- How to Declutter Your Mind: Secrets to Stop Overthinking, Relieve Anxiety, and Achieve Calmness and Inner Peace

- Beginning Zen Buddhism: Timeless Teachings to Master Your Emotions, Reduce Stress and Anxiety, and Achieve Inner Peace

- Gaslighting Recovery Workbook: How to Recognize Manipulation, Overcome Narcissistic Abuse, Let Go, and Heal from Toxic Relationships

- Empath Secrets: How to Awaken Your Superpower, Protect Yourself Against Emotional Overload, and Live an Empowered Life

- Relationship Anxiety: 7 Steps to Freedom from Jealousy, Attachment, Worry, and Fear – Heal and Rediscover Your Love for Each Other

References

Bancroft, L. (2003). *Why Does He Do That?: Inside the Minds of Angry and Controlling Men*

(Reprint ed.). Berkley Books.

Campbell, K. W., & Crist, C. (2020). *The New Science of Narcissism: Understanding One of*

the Greatest Psychological Challenges of Our Time—and What You Can Do About It

(Illustrated ed.). Sounds True.

Engel, B. (2003). *The Emotionally Abusive Relationship: How to Stop Being Abused and*

How to Stop Abusing (1st ed.). Wiley.

Hall, J. L. (2019). *Narcissist in Your Life*. Da Capo Lifelong Books.

Lcsw, S. T. (2016). *Healing from Hidden Abuse: A Journey Through the Stages of Recovery*

from Psychological Abuse. MAST Publishing House.

Lowen, A. (1985). *Narcissism: Denial of the True Self* (New edition). Touchstone.

Malkin, C. (2016). *Rethinking Narcissism: The Secret to Recognizing and Coping with*

Narcissists (Reprint ed.). Harper Perennial.

Narcissistic Abuse Recovery

MacKenzie, J., & Thomas, S. (2019). *Whole Again: Healing Your Heart and Rediscovering*

Your True Self After Toxic Relationships and Emotional Abuse. TarcherPerigee.

PsyD, E. M., & Md, S. J. (2016). *Unmasking Narcissism: A Guide to Understanding the*

Narcissist in Your Life. Althea Press.

www.ingramcontent.com/pod-product-compliance
Lightning Source LLC
Chambersburg PA
CBHW070116030426
42335CB00016B/2177